The Changing Legal World of Adolescence

Franklin E. Zimring

 THE FREE PRESS
A Division of Macmillan Publishing Co., Inc.
NEW YORK

Collier Macmillan Publishers
LONDON

The Free Press
A Division of Macmillan Publishing Co., Inc.
866 Third Avenue, New York, N.Y. 10022

Collier Macmillan Canada, Inc.

Library of Congress Catalog Card Number: 81-68475

Printed in the United States of America

printing number

1 2 3 4 5 6 7 8 9 10

Library of Congress Cataloging in Publication Data

Zimring, Franklin E.
    The changing legal world of adolescence.

    Includes index.
    1. Youth—Legal status, laws, etc.—United States.
I. Title.
KF479.Z55   346.7301′35   81-68475
ISBN 0-02-935960-0   347.306135   AACR2

This book is dedicated to my parents,
for love, guidance, and semi-autonomy.

Contents

Preface

Some years ago, as a junior professor, I inherited the "Family Law" course at the University of Chicago. While my interest in the problems of youth and juvenile justice was strong, my scholarship was concentrated in criminal law and criminal justice policy. In 1978, I wrote a small essay on the jurisprudence of youth and sent it to a friend and former teacher, Francis A. Allen. From there, a combination of supportive people and generous institutions created this book.

Professor Allen suggested expanding the essay into a series of lectures. His enthusiasm, and the kindness of his colleagues at the University of Michigan, resulted in an invitation to deliver the 30th Thomas Cooley lectures in Ann Arbor in October, 1980. Those lectures form the nucleus of this book, for which Professor Allen deserves much of the credit—and some of the blame. I am, for this and many other reasons, grateful for his guidance.

Where could I write such a book? At Chicago, I have the usual administrative duties and day-to-day concerns. An invitation to become a fellow at the Center for Advanced Studies in the Behavioral Sciences at Palo Alto, California, provided the necessary haven. During the academic year 1979–80, the Center provided a superb environment for thinking, writing, and talking to a remarkable collection of colleagues. John Walsh, one of that entourage, contributed in three ways. First, he asked penetrating questions about my own philosophy of law and legal research. Second, he inspired me to seek an audience wider than my academic peers. Finally, he was generous with his time and intellect, idea by idea, page by page. What a splendid colleague!

The list of people I imposed on is embarrassingly large: Walter Dean Burham, Ewart Thomas (who constructed formal models of parts of chapters 10 and 11), Jerome Kagan, and Paul Beneciraf at the Center; John Kaplan, Robert Mnookin and Michael Wald at Stanford; Norval Morris, James Coleman, Philip Kurland, Walter Blum, and Henry Monaghan at the University of Chicago; Francis Allen and David Chambers at the University of Michigan. Barrik Van Winkle served as combination Renaissance man/research assistant. Ladonna Deer typed with skill and dedication. I hope their time was wisely invested.

Franklin E. Zimring
Chicago, Illinois
May, 1981

Introduction

Adolescence ... The process or condition of growing up: the growing age of human beings; the period which extends from childhood to manhood or womanhood. ...

The Oxford English Dictionary (1970)

Adolescence. That age which follows puberty and precedes the age of majority.

Black's Law Dictionary (rev. 5th ed. 1979)

This work is an attempt to explain a series of recent changes in the legal conception of adolescence as a stage of life and as a transition to adulthood. My intended audience includes lawyers and others—such as parents, professionals, and kids—who have been puzzled by recent trends that have been labeled "children's liberation" and "the revolution in juvenile justice."

Changes in legal conceptions of youth are interesting in their own right. They are also a useful way of examining important social, political, and economic changes. Francis Allen has asserted that "one characteristic of legal studies, properly pursued, is that they lead to a fuller understanding of the larger world of which the law and its institutions are a part."[1] It is his conception of the law as a path to the world that motivated this essay.

The definition of adolescence quoted from Black's dictionary suggests, however, that this particular branch of the law isn't a path to much of anything. It is true that the *Law Dictionary* approach to American adolescence has virtues that no legal mind should lightly reject: certainty, simplicity, and the image of legal control. We are certain that adolescence begins at puberty and ends with a legislative judgment that the age of majority has arrived. The standards against which to judge the exit from adolescence are concrete and measurable: a single chronological age. Even more heartening, Black's definition conveys an image of control in these uncertain times. If the age of majority is the boundary of American adolescence, it can be legislatively amended. An adult is anyone the state legislature says is adult.

But life is not that simple, and the price we pay for sustaining such illusions is considerable. Adolescence, in my view, is both a period in itself and a transition. It is a term of years when those not yet adult are engaged in the process of becoming adult, a rich but often stressful period of trial and error. As a period of semi-autonomy, it places special burdens on legal reasoning and public choice. As a transition to adulthood, it demands a future orientation in public policy: How we grow up is an important determinant of what kinds of adults we grow up to be.

Further, in these last years of the twentieth century, adolescence requires a peculiar mix of liberty and order that is anything but simple to achieve. Unlike the earlier stages of childhood, this is a time when the adolescent acquires a voice and a will that we can neither ignore nor slavishly follow. In the jargon of the law library, contemporary adolescents possess "liberty interests" and voices to speak them; at the same time, they are prone to make mistakes that enlightened public policy cannot ignore in the name of civil liberty. A central theme in my analysis is that full maturity can only be achieved by what Wallace Stevens called "committing experience." But how do we get from here to there? If a person can't make choices without the experience of making choices, how can that person become an adult without being one? It is this need to learn one's way into maturity that makes growing up in a free society a process rather than an event.

As one of the distinct social roles that recent American experience has created, adolescence has attracted the attention of a wide variety of social, biological, and behavioral scientists. Psychological and sociological literature on the topic appears in staggering quantities. A search of psychological general abstracts reveals that no fewer than 4,000 journal articles have appeared on the topic, more than 1,500 since 1972. The terms adolescent and adolescence appear in the titles of over 3,500 journal articles published between 1972 and 1977 in the behavioral and social sciences.[2] The term "adolescent" has indeed become so freighted with connotation in social science that a presidential panel deliberately avoided it in presenting a report on "Youth: The Transition to Adulthood."[3] Some years before, the chairman of that panel wrote a book titled *The Adolescent Society*.[4]

Lawyers, however, speak a different language. The terms adolescence and adolescent rarely appear in the titles of our scholarly tomes. A quite creditable summary of the "Constitutional Rights of Minors" was recently written that did not mention those terms once.[5] A thousand page casebook on "Modern Juvenile Justice" does not include either adolescence or youth in its subject matter index.[6]

This semantic discontinuity is a symptom of deeper problems. The law has for the past quarter century been struggling with the implications of a crucial social stage without calling it by its rightful name. Legal labels for adolescent development are cumbersome, uninformative, and constrictive. The lawyer deals with a world inhabited by minors and adults, juveniles and non-juveniles. The crudity and artificiality of the terms have led, in some special circumstances, to even more refined "terms of art." There are special legal cubbyholes for minors who are "mature," "in need of supervision," and "not amenable to treatment."[7]

In some jurisdictions, the question of whether a 16-year-old accused of murder will stay in juvenile court, or be tried in the criminal courts for a capital crime, will depend on an individual judge assessing whether that 16-year-old is "mature" and "sophisticated." If he is found to be "sophisticated," his reward can be eligibility for the electric chair.[8]

One consequence of this linguistic discontinuity is

that law and social science have been talking past each other on issues relating to adolescence for quite some time. A second result is that legal doctrines relating to adolescence frequently appear strained and are susceptible to gross misinterpretation. My task is to provide a foundation for reinterpreting emerging legal doctrine, using common sense and ordinary language.

Preliminary warnings about the nature of my ambitions and the gospel I shall be preaching seem appropriate. The problems I shall deal with will remain unresolved at the conclusion of the last sermon. There are no easy answers to the problems of legal policy toward those engaged in a long transition to adulthood. I will be selling perspective rather than prescription, offering insights rather than cures. But it is fair to state that in my view, the role of law is to be properly reactive and relatively modest in defining and reshaping the meaning of adolescence in American society.

If all of this sounds self-effacing, let me hasten to give you a pretentious description of the perspective to be put on display: this book attempts to apply a realist jurisprudential method to the problems of law and the young. That description may be pretentious, but it is unconfining. After half a century of advocacy, the "method" of legal realist analysis remains imprecisely defined.[9] Some of this imprecision relates to the broad sweep of the basic postulates; much of the vagueness associated with realist jurisprudence stems from the fact that more time has been allocated to preachment of this approach than to its practice.

Still, legal thought has benefited greatly from the contributions of Jerome Frank, Karl Llewellyn, and their

followers.[10] The legal formalism of the treatise writers
was effectively challenged in traditional areas such as
contract, tort, and conflict of laws. Understandably, the
realists of the prior generation never got around to criti-
cally examining the institutions and assumptions that
had emerged by the turn of the century. This new body
of law, heavy with optimism about the malleability of
human nature and the benign quality of state intervention, thrived unchallenged while the formalists were
taking their lumps in the halls of academe. A more recent generation of scholars, including Francis Allen and
Norval Morris,[11] have pioneered in the critical scrutiny
of the jurisprudence of juvenile justice and rehabilitation. My goal is to follow in their footsteps.

The first part of this book surveys recent changes in
the legal regulation of adolescents and provides a short
history of the legal theory of youth that dominated
American thought through the first six decades of the
twentieth century. Part II describes the many reasons
why we have been rethinking the wholly dependent
theory of youth during the period since the mid-1960's.
Part III attempts to sketch out a revised legal theory of
growing up that is consistent with modern social reality.
Part IV speculates about the future course of adolescence in public law.

Through all of this the question persists: is the law
really a useful path to the world? Professor Allen restricted his argument to legal studies that are "properly
pursued." My argument is that closer examination of
changes in the law can indeed improve our understanding of the world in which it operates. That is the task of
the pages that follow.

Notes

1. Francis A. Allen, "The Law as a Path to the World," 77 *Michigan Law Review* 157 (1978).
2. Computer search by Carol Trainer at the Center for Advanced Studies in the Behavioral Sciences, Stanford, California, in late 1979.
3. *Youth: Transition to Adulthood*, Report of the Panel on Youth of the President's Science Advisory Committee (Washington, D.C.: Government Printing Office, 1973).
4. James Coleman, *The Adolescent Society: The Social Life of the Teenager and Its Impact on Education* (New York: Free Press of Glencoe, 1961).
5. American Law Division of the Congressional Research Service, *Constitutional Rights of Children*, 95th Congress, 2nd Session, printed for the use of the Senate Committee on the Judiciary (1978).
6. Sanford J. Fox, *Modern Juvenile Justice* (St. Paul: West Publishing Company, 1979).
7. *See, for example,* Colorado Children's Code, §22-1-3(19) (a) (d) (e); McKinney's New York Family Court Act, §312(b); Georgia Code Annotated, §24-2408(4) (Supplement 1969); Illinois Juvenile Court Act, §702-5; West's Annual California Welfare and Institutional Code, §601.
8. *See* the Appendix to *Kent v. United States,* 383 U.S. 541, at 565-568; Franklin E. Zimring, *Confronting Youth Crime,* Report of the Twentieth Century Fund Task Force on Sentencing Policy Toward Young Offenders (New York: Holmes & Meier, 1978) at 95–104; and Franklin E. Zimring, "Notes Toward a Jurisprudence of Waiver," in *Major Issues in Juvenile Justice Information and Training: Readings in Public Policy,* John C. Hall, Donna Martin Hamparian, John M. Pettibone & Joseph L. White, eds. (Columbus, Ohio: Academy for Contemporary Problems, 1981).

9. *See* Francis A. Allen, "Views from the Forties: Jerome Frank's *Law and the Modern Mind*," in Allen, *Law, Intellect, and Education* (Ann Arbor: University of Michigan Press, 1979) at 17–22.

10. *See, for example,* Jerome Frank, *Law and the Modern Mind* (New York: Doubleday, 1930); Jerome Frank and Barbara Frank, *Not Guilty* (Garden City, N.Y.: Doubleday, 1957); Karl Llewellyn and E. Adamson Hoebel, *The Cheyenne Way* (Norman: University of Oklahoma Press, 1941); Jerome Hall, *Theft, Law and Society* (Boston: Little, Brown & Co., 1935).

11. Francis A. Allen, *The Borderland of Criminal Justice* (Chicago: University of Chicago Press, 1964); Norval Morris, *The Future of Imprisonment* (Chicago: University of Chicago Press, 1974) especially Chapter 2, "Rehabilitating the 'Rehabilitative Ideal'."

Part I:

What's Going On Here?

Things like this make the newspapers:

> Item: *A 15-year-old sues her parents for "divorce" and the judge rules in her favor.*
>
> Item: *Researchers win a federal grant to study the motives and "lifestyles" of adolescent and preadolescent prostitutes, some as young as 10 or 11 years of age.*
>
> Item: *High school graduates sue the local school board for "educational malpractice" because they can't read adequately while teachers complain they are frequently assaulted in the same kind of schools.*
>
> Item: *Clinics open to provide 12- and 13-year-old girls with birth control information—no questions are asked and no parents are told.*
>
> More Items: *Schools for truants close as truancy increases; homes for unwed mothers go unoccupied while unwed motherhood skyrockets; illegal drug use among adolescents becomes so prevalent it is used as an argument for removing the criminal law from these forms of adolescent behavior.*

As usual, the papers don't tell the whole story. The real changes we are witnessing in the social and legal facts of American adolescence are deeper and different. What appear to be massive and sudden changes are not so big and not so quick. The law, notwithstanding judicial activism, has been following rather than leading social redefinition of the teen years. Yet the relation between the state and its older children—who happen also to be our children and those of our friends—has indisputably entered a state of transition.

Change, of course, is inevitable. But the law should understand itself and be prepared to explain itself. What has happened and is happening to the legal status of the young should make sense to them as well as to their elders. I begin this book with three chapters that lay the foundation for understanding the recent past and probable future of the changing legal world of adolescence. Chapter 1 presents four case studies in the legal world of growing up and provides the reader with an introduction to the legal reasoning, frequently misguided, that has accompanied trends variously labeled as "children's liberation" and "the revolution in juvenile justice." Chapter 2 examines two simple arguments often advanced to explain recent changes: earlier maturity among the young and the discovery of a "children's rights" movement much like those that have expanded civil rights to minorities and women. Chapter 3 briefly explores the recent historical movement to treat adolescents differently. It discusses the images of children that created a special legal world of childhood at the turn of the century as well as some more recent social forces that exerted pressure on earlier stereotypes while the jurisprudence of youth remained stagnant. All of this sets the stage for one man's analysis of what has happened in recent years—and why—as discussed in Part II.

1

Four Case Studies in Confusion

How Old Is Old Enough to Drink?

In 1971, the Michigan legislature lowered the minimum age for purchasing alcoholic beverages from the twenty-first to the eighteenth birthday. This adjustment was a response to the Twenty-sixth Amendment to the Constitution, which made a parallel downward shift in the minimum age for exercising the franchise. In 1978, however, Michigan voters, in a binding referendum, raised the drinking age back to a minimum of 21. And in 1980, the electorate soundly defeated a proposal to lower the minimum age, this time to the nineteenth birthday. After decades of legislative inaction, Michigan lawmakers and voters were required to

3

decide about minimum drinking ages three times in less than ten years, and to choose among three different minimum ages.

There is here a related irony: twice within two years, 19- and 20-year-old citizens of Michigan were permitted to exercise their judgment about whether they should be permitted to drink, but each time this small minority was overwhelmed by the rest of the electorate.

Michigan's struggle with the drinking age question is not an isolated event. Between 1970 and 1975, a majority of the states lowered the minimum age for alcohol consumption. By the end of the decade, eight states had changed policies again, this time increasing the minimum age for purchase, and producing a chaotic pattern.

At present, thirty-nine states have adopted one of four different drinking ages (Figure 1.1). Eleven states and the District of Columbia have two different ages for different beverages. Only thirteen states agree on any single policy.

Is this arbitrary pattern fair? If citizens are old enough to vote aren't they old enough to drink? Can you imagine how we would respond to a proposal denying any other group of enfranchised citizens the right to buy a drink—for instance blacks, senior citizens, or women? If *that* kind of discrimination is unthinkable, what about *this* kind of age discrimination?

Sorting through the arguments for raising the drinking age does not put matters to rest. Studies show that lowering the drinking age increased traffic fatalities somewhat among younger drivers, but the statistics also reveal that traffic fatalities among persons under 21 were lower than those of young adults between 21 and

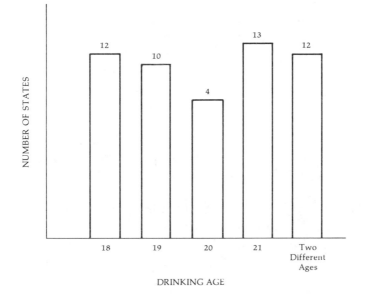

Figure 1-1 Distribution of minimum age for purchase of alcoholic beverages, 50 states and the District of Columbia, 1979.

SOURCE: Henry Wechsler & Edward S. Sands, "Minimum-Age Laws and Youthful Drinking: An Introduction," in *Minimum-Age-Drinking Laws: An Evaluation 1* (H. Wechsler, ed. 1980), at pp. 2–3.

25.[1] So why not raise the drinking age to 25? Why not prohibition for everybody?

Evidence was presented that high school students under 18 drink more when the drinking age is lowered from 21 to 18 even though this behavior is illegal. But why should we punish all 18-year-olds who wish to drink because some of them, and their younger friends, violate the law? Can't we use the same logic to prohibit purchase for those between 21 and 25 for fear they will corrupt *their* younger friends?

And speaking of logic, how should we go about making distinctions of this kind? Majority vote? Flipping coins? Or should we leave it to the experts? If so, what kind of experts and what can they tell us?

When Should Children Outgrow "Child Support"?

Growing up is much more straightforward in California. Prior to March of 1972, parents had the duty to support their minor children until the age of majority and California's age of majority was 21. When divorces occurred, the Superior Court could order a noncustodial parent to provide support and college tuition in appropriate cases until a child's twenty-first birthday.[2] This legal provision dealt with an important issue. The number of young people who desire college education is large and the cost of a college education is high. Further, divorce rates have increased substantially in California—and the rest of the United States. What, then, happened in California that caused the legislature to reconsider the issue of the power of courts to order college support?

What happened, evidently, was the voting rights amendment. The crazy-quilt logic of treating voting young adults as dependent waifs persuaded the California legislature to reduce the age of majority to the eighteenth birthday. Now California courts lack jurisdiction to provide support past age 18 to children of divorce.

One can imagine that certain hardships will result when this rule is applied in our complex and education-centered society, but the logic of the California legislation is clear, perhaps compellingly clear. Extending voting rights is a recognition of maturity. If young people are mature at 18, that birthday should mark the age of majority. If a young person has passed the age of majority, there is and should be no basis for continuing to compel parents to provide support. Of course there are young people who lack the resources to finance college education at 18 or 19, but how do they differ from equally needy offspring who are 21 or 22, or 30?

Once a societal decision is made to reduce the age at which liberty is extended, doesn't consistency require us to lower the age at which our children grow up into the responsibility of fending for themselves? And if we do not use a single age of majority to serve as the boundary between childhood dependence and adult responsibility, how can we make intelligible decisions about when adult rights and responsibilities commence?

Should Kids Have the "Right" to Purchase Contraceptives?

While the states have been struggling with the boundaries of adolescence as a transition to adulthood, the Federal Courts have been constructing a monumentally confusing constitutional law of adolescence that appears to many to have radically altered the relationship between child, parent, and state. If these adjectives seem strong, consider the case of *Carey v. Population Services International*, decided by the Supreme Court of the United States in 1976.[3] By statute, the State of New York made it a criminal offense to distribute nonprescription contraceptives to children under 16 years of age. Seven of the nine justices participating in this decision agreed that the New York law violated the Constitution because parents have rights to procure contraceptives for their children even though the use of such contraceptives by the children might be unlawful. Parents who provide children with pornographic literature can probably be prosecuted for contributing to the delinquency of a minor. This is apparently not the case with respect to contraceptives.

The members of the Court disagreed on why the New York prohibition violated the supreme law of the land. Justice Brennan, writing for himself and three Brethren, argued that the law violated privacy rights of young persons under 16. This opinion, said its author, "proceeds on the assumption that the Constitution does not bar state regulation of the sexual behavior of minors." However, earlier decisions had struck down laws requiring all unmarried minors to secure parental consent for abortions, and these cases were viewed as controlling the question of "contraceptive privacy":

> Since the State may not impose a blanket pro-hibition, or even a blanket requirement of parental consent, on the choice of a minor to terminate her pregnancy, the constitutionality of a blanket prohi-bition of the distribution of contraceptives to minors is a fortiori foreclosed.[4]

Justice Rehnquist, dissenting, argued adamantly that the due process clause of the Fourteenth Amendment to the Constitution does not provide support for striking down the New York ban on contraceptive sales to minors:

> The majority of New York's citizens are in effect told that however deeply they may be concerned about the problem of promiscuous sex and intercourse among unmarried teenagers, they may not adopt this means of dealing with it. The Court holds that New York may not use its police power to legislate in the interests of its concept of the public morality as it pertains to minors. The Court's denial of a power so fundamental to self-government must, in the long run, prove to be but a temporary departure from a wise and heretofore settled course of adjudication to the contrary.[5]

Indeed,

> The post-Civil War Congresses which drafted the Civil War Amendments to the Constitution could not have accomplished their task without the blood of brave men on both sides which was shed at Shiloh, Gettysburg, and Cold Harbor. If those responsible for these Amendments, by feats of valor or efforts of draftsmanship, could have lived to know that their efforts had enshrined in the Constitution the right of commercial vendors of contraceptives to peddle them to unmarried minors through such means as window displays and vending machines located in the men's room of truck stops, notwithstanding the considered judgment of the New York Legislature to the contrary, it is not difficult to imagine their reaction.[6]

Justice Stevens, one of three members of the Court who voted to strike down the ban but did not agree with the Brennan opinion, provides his own reasons:

> Common sense indicates that many young people will engage in sexual activity regardless of what the New York Legislature does; and further, that the incidence of venereal disease and premarital pregnancy is affected by the availability or unavailability of contraceptives. Although young persons theoretically may avoid those harms by practicing total abstention, inevitably many will not. The statutory prohibition denies them and their parents a choice which, if available, would reduce their exposure to disease or unwanted pregnancy.[7]

Under such circumstances, the attempt to ban contraceptives is defective because it attempts to teach the wrongfulness of sexual behavior using inappropriate methods,

> It is as though a State decided to dramatize its disapproval of motorcycles by forbidding the use of safety helmets. One need not posit a constitutional right to ride a motorcycle to characterize such a restriction as irrational and perverse.[8]

The list of perplexities generated by a case like *Carey* is stunningly large, but two questions in particular merit preliminary consideration. First, is it correct to conclude from a decision striking down this New York legislation that a 15-year-old has a constitutional right to condoms and vaginal foam? If so, where did the "right" come from and how many other such constitutional rights can we infer from cases like this?

Second, it is fair to ask what constitutional theory

of adolescence would allow New York to pass laws that forbid the young both sex and pornography but not contraceptives. If the 15-year-old girl has "privacy rights" to contraceptives, why can she be classified a juvenile delinquent if she puts contraceptives to their intended use?

Does a Curfew Ordinance Violate the Constitution?

One final introductory problem illustrates both the temper of our times and the complexity of the subject. Middletown, Pennsylvania, like thousands of other municipalities in the western world, uses a "nocturnal curfew" statute to prohibit children and younger adolescents from walking the streets at night without parental or other adult supervision. In Middletown, kids under 12 cannot remain unsupervised after 10:00 p.m., 12- and 13-year-olds can stay on the streets until 10:30, and 14- through 17-year-olds face an 11:00 p.m. curfew. There are a number of exceptions provided by the Middletown ordinance for situations involving adult supervision and special permissions for religious or political events.

In 1975, Shawn Bykofsky, then age 12, and his mother Joanne brought suit asking a federal court to declare the statute a violation of Shawn's and his mother's constitutional rights.

The complaint in Bykofsky alleged seven separate constitutional objections to Middletown's curfew, including charges that curfew infringed on Shawn's rights of:

1. "freedom of movement to go where one pleases,"
2. "freedom of speech, freedom of association and freedom of assembly," and
3. "freedom of travel."

In addition, Shawn's mother argued that the curfew "impermissibly encroaches on the . . . right of parents to direct the upbringing of their children and violates the constitutional guarantee of family autonomy."[9] Finally, both Shawn and his mother argued that the arbitrary age distinctions drawn by the statute deprive young persons and their parents of equal protection of the laws as granted by the Fourteenth Amendment to the Constitution.

Facing this formidable collection of arguments, the District Court judge justified the curfew as a method of protecting youngsters from the harm that might come to them from others at the same time that it supresses the crimes and "nocturnal mischief" that kids themselves might otherwise commit. The District Court thus upheld the statute and the Circuit Court of Appeals affirmed that decision without a published opinion. The United States Supreme Court declined to review this ruling by the narrowest of margins. Three justices voted to grant the writ: Mr. Justice Marshall joined by Justice Brennan wrote an opinion indicating "this case poses a substantial constitutional question. . . ."

> . . . I have little doubt but that, absent a genuine emergency, . . . a curfew aimed at all citizens could not survive constitutional scrutiny. This is true even though such a general curfew, like the instant ordinance, would protect those subject to it

from injury and prevent them from causing "nocturnal mischief."

The question squarely presented by this case, then, is whether the due process rights of juveniles are entitled to lesser protection than those of adults. The prior decisions of this Court provide no clear answer. We have recognized that "[c]onstitutional rights do not mature and come into being magically only when one attains the state-defined age of majority. Minors, as well as adults, are protected by the Constitution and possess constitutional rights. . . ." But we also have acknowledged that the State has somewhat broader authority to regulate the activities of children than of adults.[10]

The legal and historical puzzles of Shawn Bykofsky's case against curfew merit close attention. Does this case present a substantial constitutional question? If so, is it the same kind of constitutional question that the Supreme Court wrestled with in *Carey v. Population Services International?* After all, if 12-year-olds have constitutional rights to contraceptives, why shouldn't Shawn be permitted to exercise his liberty interests on an unsupervised midnight stroll? Is Mr. Justice Marshall correct when he suggests the issue is whether the due process rights of kids "are entitled to lesser protection than adults"?

The historical puzzle is this: Juvenile curfews have been a staple social regulation of the young in thousands of cities for a long time. The first federal court challenge to juvenile curfews was filed in the 1970's. If curfews are rank discrimination against the young, why did it take the Civil Rights Bar so long to raise the issue? On the other hand, what aspects of our recent history produced cases like Bykofsky?

These four case studies are part of a larger pattern of legislative and judicial activity that has been characterized as a revolution in juvenile justice. Before 1966, the United States Supreme Court had never decided a case that could properly be filed under the rubric of "juvenile rights"; in the last fifteen years, adolescence has been a major concern of the Court. The United States Reports are filled with cases adjudicating the rights of adolescents in matters as diverse as abortion, school suspension, involuntary civil commitment, corporal punishment, jury trials in juvenile court, and political demonstrations.

Federal district courts are flooded with constitutional challenges to regulations of the young that have previously gone unchallenged. Legislative bodies, state and federal, are rethinking public policy toward adolescent work and wages, compulsory education, access to medical care, and the jurisdiction and mission of the juvenile court. The American Bar Association has sponsored a Juvenile Justice Standards Project which produced no fewer than *twenty-four volumes* of suggested reforms in juvenile justice.[11]

Our four problem cases will serve as a point of reference as we review a large number of changes in the legal fabric of adolescence. To understand the issues in these cases is an important step toward comprehending the rapid and thorough re-examination of the legal status of the young. But the road to understanding is not short. Easy answers prove ultimately unacceptable, as I will argue in the following chapter and a brief history of the legal conception of adolescence is necessary to understand the institutions that emerged at the turn of the century and became the focus for reform efforts. This is the task of Chapter 3.

Notes

1. *See* Richard L. Douglas, "The Legal Drinking Age and Traffic Casualties: A Special Case of Changing Alcohol Availability in a Public Health Context," in *Minimum-Age-Drinking Laws: An Evaluation*, Henry Wechsler, ed. (Lexington, Mass.: D. C. Heath & Co., 1980) at 93. For traffic fatalities, *see* U.S. Bureau of the Census, *Statistical Abstract of the United States*, from 1945 onwards in variously titled sections on traffic fatalities.

2. *Compare* California Civil Code (1971) §25.1 (West) *with* California Civil Code (1972) §25.1 (West).

3. *Carey v. Population Services International*, 431 U.S. 678 (1976).

4. *Carey*, 431 U.S. 678, at 694 (1976).

5. *Carey*, 431 U.S. 678, at 719 (Rehnquist, J., dissenting.)

6. *Carey*, 431 U.S. 678, at 717–18 (1976) (Rehnquist, J. dissenting).

7. *Carey*, 431 U.S. 678, at 714 (1976) (Stevens, J., concurring in part).

8. *Carey*, 431 U.S. 678, at 715 (1976) (Stevens, J., concurring in part).

9. *Bykofsky v. Middletown*, 401 F. Supp. 1242 (1975).

10. *Bykofsky v. Middletown*, 429 U.S. 964, at 965 (Marshall, J., dissenting from denial of *certiorari*).

11. Institute of Judicial Administration/American Bar Association, Juvenile Justice Standards Project (Tentative Draft 1977).

2

Are Kids Different?

> . . . The only part of the conduct of any one, for which he is amenable to society, is that which concerns others. In the part which merely concerns himself, his independence is, of right, absolute. Over himself, over his own body and mind, the individual is sovereign.
>
> It is, perhaps, hardly necessary to say that this doctrine is meant to apply only to human beings in the maturity of their faculties. We are not speaking of children, or of young persons below the age which the law may fix as that of manhood or womanhood. Those who are still in a state to require being taken care of by others, must be protected against their own actions as well as external injury.

J. S. Mill,
On Liberty

I'm a goddamned minor.

Holden Caulfield,
The Catcher in the Rye

Mr. Mill, the eminent civil libertarian, thinks kids are different when it comes to the question of individual liberty. And his reservations extend not only to small children but also to those "young persons below the age which the law may fix as that of manhood or womanhood." Mr. Caulfield, perhaps the most celebrated adolescent of this literary century, resents the paternalism that restricts his freedom of choice as he roams New York, 6 feet tall but only 16. In the closing decades of the twentieth century it is no longer "hardly necessary" to say that doctrines of liberty are not meant to apply to the young.

Instead, there is controversy both about what age is the proper boundary to "manhood or womanhood" and what restrictions can properly be placed on those who are engaged in the transitional period of adolescence. Indeed, many would argue that my four case studies and most of the other changes we will examine are the outgrowth of two uncomplicated trends: legal recognition of earlier maturity, and a phenomenon known as children's liberation. At the outset, it might be helpful to explore these explanations in an effort to see whether these two popular labels accurately describe the changing social and legal world of adolescence. Simple answers, after all, are preferable to complicated ones, even in an age of computers and model-building.

Early Maturity

The simple explanation for extending the franchise to 18-year-olds while denying the possibility of economic support in California is that kids are growing up faster these days and therefore "becoming adult" at an earlier age. In this view, a single age of majority should mark the boundary between childhood and adulthood for all purposes, and Michigan's decision to deny those under 21 the right to purchase alcohol, for example, is an obvious mistake. This method of public policy analysis is simple and straightforward; duly advised by *Black's Law Dictionary*, we consult the statute books to discover the single age of majority and confer all adult privileges on that birthday. That magic birthday is 18 and will remain so as long as the voting age is not reduced. (History tells us emphatically that the age will not be increased within our current constitutional framework. Extending the franchise is relatively easy. Disenfranchising any group would not only require, but would constitute, an American counterrevolution.)

Are kids becoming adult earlier? Will a single birthday suffice? And should it be age 18? Extending the franchise to 18-year-olds was a justifiable accommodation of youth that produced no discernable social harm and did not infringe on youth welfare. Eighteen-year-olds can vote or refuse to vote. They can vote Democratic this year and Republican the next. Young people, collectively, run the risk of making irreversible mistakes only in those areas where persons under 21 constitute a very large percentage of eligible voters. The extension of the franchise has few obvious or significant costs.

This is important because of the contrast between absolute and relative development that characterizes the career of many modern adolescents: the 18-year-old of 1981 typically has achieved more in terms of formal education than the 18-year-old of 1900, but he or she typically has further to go to complete the process. The absolute advantage of the modern adolescent is an argument for earlier exercise of privileges that depend on minimal competence. On a relative basis, however, intellectual and social development is no greater for today's 18- or 17- or 15-year-old than for his ancestor in the earlier years of this century. *Kids have come further, but they have further to go.* This juxtaposition of absolute and relative accomplishment is of some importance to public policy; it is particularly troublesome when adolescent decisions or public decisions about adolescents may have permanent consequences.

California's ambidextrous use of a single age of majority is a good illustration of the problem. For those who pursue higher education—an increasing proportion of the population—the period of economic dependency has lengthened considerably. The number of 18- through 21-year-olds in post-secondary education has increased from 15 percent in 1940 to 32 percent in 1978.[1] Whatever the basis for legally decreasing the age of parental liability for education expenses, it is not that adolescents have achieved greater economic independence by their late teen years.

Another, and striking, illustration of the problem concerns public perception of readiness for parenthood. Today, teenage pregnancy is regarded as a substantial national problem. Public alarm is expressed not merely about out-of-wedlock pregnancy and pregnancy in the early teens, but also about married 18- and 19-year-old women having babies. The incidence of childbearing in this age group has not increased recently; indeed, the birthrate is down from the "baby boom" years of the 1950's, even though illegitimate births have increased.[2]

What's wrong with women under 20 having babies? A comprehensive explanation comes from a recent study of teenage marriage.

> What are the social and demographic implications of teenage marriages? A teenage marriage may short-circuit a woman's chance to develop a role alternate to that of housewifery and motherhood. The more teenage women who are married, the more pressure there will be for family-building activity, and the more important will be the other social problems associated with teenage marriages.
>
> The crux of the question of early marriage lies in the birth of children. If no children were born, no health problems associated with children of young mothers would develop. If no children were born, divorce would create no difficulties in the maintenance, socialization, and social placement of children. If no children were born, no contribution would be made by teenage marriages to the nation's birth rate.
>
> Marriage contributes to the problem of fertility by providing a socially acceptable outlet for childbearing, and being an inherently pronatalist institution in which the young bride and mother finds encouragement and reinforcement for continued childbearing. But even if no children are born immediately, teenage marriages may have dubious consequences. They may interrupt or cut off a teenager's chance for more education, a better job, and perhaps an input into increasing the quality of life in American society.[3]

Many of the author's arguments resemble a general assault on marriage. Whenever a woman marries, this increases the chances of her becoming a "housewife," and whenever marriage occurs it provides "a socially acceptable outlet for childbearing." This, presumably, "contributies to the problem of fertility" whether the mother is 18 or 28. Divorce rates are higher among the young, but they are also high for the general population. And the health problems associated with childbearing in the late teens are probably less serious than those encountered by pregnancies after 30.[4]

Yet the heart of the argument is that early parenthood interrupts the parent's process of development and impinges on future choices and life chances. Having and keeping a child locks an 18-year-old parent into duties and forecloses opportunities. This sense of arrested development must, in turn, reflect a perception that the middle and late teen years are a period when young people still face the unfinished business of growing up.

Teenage pregnancy and prolonged economic dependence are not the only special problems we presently associate with youth. Each month, the Department of Labor publishes separate statistics on teenage unemployment. While this is only one of several special categories—breadwinners, women, and blacks are also given special reports—the teenage statistics have a life, or a lifelessness, of their own. Prospective workers under 21 lag significantly behind their elders in the competition for jobs of any kind, and particularly for skilled jobs.[5] Black young men suffer rates of unemployment that should inspire statistical nostalgia for the Great Depression.[6] Why is this so, and what should we make of it?

I find all of these data indicative of a deeper fact:

our children remain not fully adult for years beyond high school. The period of not-quite-adulthood extends longer now than before. Even the Army advertises its opportunities as a training program for the late teens rather than a job. High school graduates, first pictured as being turned down by the civilian world for lack of "experience" are told the Army is the place to find that magic passage to adulthood. The Navy tells our kids it is the path to missile launchers rather than McDonalds. The Marine Corps still insists it is looking for a "few good men," but its advertising agency explicitly depicts being a Marine as the process of becoming a man. From Harvard to Harlem, rites of passage take longer in the United States of the 1980's.

None of this, of course, provides direct guidance on issues such as the proper legal minimum age for voting, drinking, driving, signing contracts or settling down. This early in the argument, I wish to suggest only one conclusion: Recent generations of American youth have not achieved an across-the-board precociousness that could explain an all-encompassing downward shift in the age when peers, parents, and the public should expect full adult status to be achieved. We cannot look to the social facts of youth to explain a comprehensive decline in the age of majority. Further, it is unwise to suppose that elected officials can, an any real sense, legislate full maturity simply by changing the law. This is unfortunate, perhaps, but nonetheless true.

Children's Liberation

There is a second simple answer implicit in recent scholarly discussions of cases like *Carey v. Population Services* and Shawn Bykofsky's constitutional assault on

curfew laws. In caricature, this perspective is the bed-
time story of the 1990's. first there was black liberation,
then there was women's liberation, then there was children's liberation.

My first quibble with that oversimplified portrait is
definitional: the legal adjustments we will be examining
are importantly centered in adolescence rather than in
the larger and more diverse universe of American
childhood. There are, I am aware, advocates of extending adult-like rights to very young children. Richard
Farson, author of a far-reaching "Children's Bill of
Rights" proposal, argues that children should achieve
"full civil rights . . . at birth, perhaps even a few months
earlier" rather than attempt to set "an arbitrary age of
competence."[7] In his view, the recognition of adoles
cent self-determination is simply one step toward a system where children of almost all ages are fully and
equally autonomous. History may judge this view to be
correct, though I doubt it.

But current debates about runaways, abortion, contraception, school dress codes, and curfew concern the
adolescent years. Just as our older children are different
from adults, they differ also from their younger siblings.
It would be remarkable indeed if the same public policy
was appropriate for 6-year-olds and 16-year-olds. It is,
as we have already seen, difficult to use what Dr. Farson calls an "arbitrary age of competence." But it would
be foolhardy to ignore the wide range of developmental
differences that span the years of childhood.

My second objection to viewing recent changes as
an extension of the Civil Rights and Women's Rights
movements concerns the ultimate goal of liberation. The
Civil Rights paradigm of the 1960's was equality. The
central meaning of this equality can be briefly stated: the

law should be color blind. Whatever the transitional difficulties of achieving equality of opportunity, the legal world we are pursuing is one in which black people are no different from white people.

The agonies of our debate on Affirmative Action mask a deeper social consensus. The Affirmative Action dispute is about means rather than ends. It is a debate about whether a color-conscious present is necessary or permissible in attempting to achieve a color-blind future. In the world we are striving for, race and ethnicity will not matter in the eyes of the law.

Unless I am mistaken, equality in the eyes of the law is the stated aim of the Women's Movement as well. The fundamental civil right pursued is freedom of choice in making life decisions, unencumbered by legal restraints that freeze persons into roles determined by gender. Putting aside the thorny questions of what equality means in a world where only women can become pregnant and have babies, the legal agenda of the Women's Movement builds toward roles that are gender blind.

The desirability of a legal order that is totally "gender blind" is in dispute for reasons not unrelated to our consideration of adolescence. Much of the legislation in this country that makes gender a decisive criterion was passed with a protective purpose or rationale. Opponents of equal rights argue the detriment of equal burdens. The specter of women in combat alarms many who are comfortable with traditional female roles, and many of those people are women. But the price of protection has been unjustifiably high in the labor market, the academy, and the corridors of governmental power. The paternalism of much gender-specific legislation

represented immutable, lifelong barriers as well as protection. The artificial barriers must fall. Whether this
should or can lead to a gender-blind legal system is one
of the great issues of our age, at present unresolved.

But if I am correct in asserting that the proper
paradigm on matters of race and sex has been equality,
then the analogy between these movements and the
changing legal world of adolescence is incomplete. The
only way to construct a jurisprudence of equality in
adolescence is to rob the adolescent years of any special
legal meaning. The test question, then, is whether we
are trying to build toward a world in which 14- or 15-
year-olds are treated no differently by the law because
they are 14 or 15—a "youth-blind" legal order. Do we
wish to abolish youth as a legally relevant concept and
let the entire transition from childhood dependence to
full adulthood occur on a single birthday?

It is, I would argue, preposterous to attempt to answer that question by consulting our attitudes on racial
equality, on the proper legal role of gender, or on compulsory retirement ages. The costs and benefits of
American adolescence deserve their own special consideration.

At the same time, other forms of liberation have
influenced the recent changes in legal policy toward
youth. The young have strong interests in liberty that
have been illuminated and advanced by the developing
moral sensitivity of the prior two decades. The social
forces that shaped and were shaped by other civil rights
movements have contributed to the climate for rethinking adolescence. Many of the same forces that push
toward equality in matters of race and sex have led us to
the recognition that even unfinished or imperfect beings

have interests in liberty. Without attempting to stig-
matize the adolescent experience by association, I think
we can see meaningful parallels in the movements that
advance the interests of prisoners, the mentally handicapped, the physically handicapped, the mentally ill,
and the aged.

Heightened respect for human rights has meant, in
such cases, that even if the law must treat individuals
differently by reason of incapacity, it must limit liberty
in the least restrictive way necessary to secure the needs
of the wider community and the specially treated class.
This whole notion of the "least restrictive alternative"[8]
is based on the long delayed insight that a legally relevant incapacity or defect does not strip one of all per-
sonhood or autonomy in the eyes of the law.

But why lump adolescence with the litany of impediments just discussed? Why *not* equality? Is there
not an uncanny parallel between the "protective legislation" women see as oppressive and the dependent
status, with burdens as well as benefits, that denial of a
jurisprudence of equality would allow? Cannot government then be used to punish the young, a fear-
inducing and relatively powerless minority group in our
society? These are questions not easily answered.

There are, however, two considerations specific to
adolescence which cannot be lightly dismissed. First,
there may be benefit in a special, legally protected growing period that is a transition to a fully realized adult
status. Privileges may be extended earlier if some residual capacity for control is retained. We might, for
example, grant the privilege to drive at an earlier age
because we can restrict, to some extent, adolescent
drinking. We are also much more likely to support edu-

cation and work training if we give adolescence special meaning.

Second, the burdens imposed during adolescence will be outgrown. Except when a nation's young people are called to war (and this may require special dispensation) legal regulation applying specifically to the young can properly be viewed as postponing rather than denying the exercise of liberty. To say to a black man that he cannot drink until he is white, or to a woman that she cannot serve in the Armed Forces until she is a man, is quite different from announcing that 18-year-olds cannot drink until they are 21. Age-related prohibitions may seem like forever to the subjects of the regulation, but they are not.

Thus, simple-minded reasoning by analogy is both misleading and unpersuasive. Even the newly popular concept of "age discrimination" sweeps too broadly when it encompasses adolescence and compulsory retirement. Barring reincarnation, if you are 66 years old you are never going to be 65 again. But we have every reason to shape policies on the assumption that our 15-year-olds will, after six years or so, turn 21.

The alternatives to such an assumption are frightening enough to push us toward a semi-autonomous view of the young. Complete emancipation of young persons at 12 or 13 is either legal fiction or utopian fantasy, ill-suited to the real world of the teen years. Failure to recognize any claims to liberty until the magic birthday of majority is a profoundly illiberal policy that is out of step with legal and social conditions of our age. Indeed, the theory that those who are not totally independent should be regarded as totally dependent is the most troublesome aspect of the legal theory of early adolescence associated with juvenile courts, public schools, and social services for most of this century. These earlier assumptions about youth welfare merit examination both as a history of earlier reform and as an explanation of why the "revolution" in juvenile justice has occurred. Those who would prefer a more clear-cut image of adolescent rights and responsibilities will find, in our recent past, a theory of youth that was consistent, coherent and, for the most part, wrong.

Notes

1. *See Youth: Transition to Adulthood*, Report of the Panel on Youth of the President's Science Advisory Committee (Washington, D.C.: Government Printing Office, 1973) at 76; Bureau of the Census, *Current Population Reports*, Series P-20, Number 346 (1979) at 11.
2. *See* the 1964 edition of *Vital Statistics of the United States* (*Natality*) for a historical series of childbirth statistics. For later years see the annual volumes thereafter.
3. John R. Weeks, *Teenage Marriages: A Demographic Analysis* (Westport, Conn.: Greenwood Press, 1976) at 3.
4. In 1976, for example, the maternal death rate per 100,000 live births was 6.8 for women under 20 and 17.9 for women ages 30–34. *See Vital Statistics of the United States* (*Mortality, Part A*) (1976) at 73.
5. *See* Bureau of Labor Statistics, *Handbook of Labor Statistics* (Bulletin 2020, 1980) at 74–77.
6. In 1979 unemployment of black males ages 16 to 20 was 34.1 percent. This rate does not, however, take into account those persons not in the labor market who are not in school. *See* Bureau of Labor Statistics, *Handbook of Labor Statistics* (Bulletin 2020, 1980) at 71. The unemployment

rate at the height of the depression in 1933 was 24.9 percent, *see* Bureau of the Census, *Historical Statistics of the United States—Colonial Times to 1970* (1975) at 135.

7. Richard Farson, The Children's Rights Movement, in *The Future of Childhood and Juvenile Justice*, Lamar T. Empey, ed. (Charlottesville: University Press of Virginia, 1979) at 55. *See also* Richard Farson, *Birthrights* (New York: Macmillan, 1974).

8. For a discussion of the "least restrictive alternative" in the context of juvenile justice, *see* Institute of Judicial Administration/American Bar Association, Juvenile Justice Standards Project, *Standards Relating to Disposition, Tentative Draft* (Cambridge, Mass.: Ballinger Publishing Co., 1977) at 34–38.

3

Childhood and Public Law Before the Revolution

When a comprehensive history of the United States in the 1970's is written, it will report that in 1974 Congress passed a law designed to persuade the States that 14- and 15-year-old boys and girls should not be detained in secure institutions that much resemble prisons because they disobey their parents or absent themselves from school.[1] Implementation of this legislation proved controversial.

That law, and many other recent reforms, cannot be comprehended without reference to the theories and institutions that preceded it. How did it come to pass that children who disobey their parents could be locked up in "state training schools"? What legal theory of adolescence could justify such an intervention? What kind of policy was being pursued? The theory was one of public responsibility for childhood dependency. The policy being pursued was the welfare of children. This theory of state responsibility was a liberal reform, widely acclaimed and pursued with sincerity by a number of admirable figures.

This chapter will argue that recent changes in law were a delayed reaction to changes in the social meaning of adolescence. I begin by describing briefly the institutions and mission of the child-saving movement at the turn of the century, passing next to the theory of youth that supported these reforms, the "jurisprudence of juvenility." Finally, I survey the changes in the social meanings of adolescence that forced the legal reforms of recent years.

Child Saving

The formal justification for the child protective reforms of the early twentieth century was a doctrine of *parens patriae*, a construction only loosely related to earlier common law doctrine.[2] This new theory, dominant for most of the twentieth century, rested on three postulates:

that childhood is a period of dependency and risk in which supervision is essential for survival;

that the family is of primary importance in the supervision of children, but the state should play a primary role in the education of children and intervene forcefully whenever the family setting fails to provide adequate nurture, moral training, or supervision; and

that when a child is at risk, the appropriate authority to decide what is in the child's best interest is a public official.

The institutions that gave expression to this theory included public schools, juvenile courts, public and private agencies of philanthropy, youth groups such as the Boy Scouts, and institutions for the housing and training of the young. Most of these institutions had historical antecedents, but the public optimism of the "progressive era" provided a mandate for expansion and change. Some form of public grade school education was common at the turn of the century, but fewer than 7 percent of all 17 year old's graduated from high school in 1900.[3] Juvenile reformatories and child-oriented urban philanthropic outposts had an impressive nineteenth century pedigree.

New legislation gave these institutions a twentieth century mandate and a legitimating legal philosophy. Public institutions were to provide what boys and girls needed: training and control. The public common school was to provide basic training; soon, the public high school was enlisted as a supplement and the age of compulsory education was increased. By 1940, 51 percent of all adolescents finished high school; by 1960 the percentage had increased to 63.[4]

The Juvenile Court was to pursue child welfare when children were at risk by using the agencies of state government to ensure that "the care, custody and discipline of the child shall approximate... that which should be given by its parents."[5] This most famous excerpt from the Juvenile Court Act of 1899 was the goal of the new state role in child rearing.

Public schools, public values, parents, and voluntary agencies would get the job done in most cases. When these institutions were insufficient to the task, the Juvenile Court would intervene.

This new court for children was granted jurisdiction in cases where minors were found to be neglected, dependent, or delinquent. If a child was at risk and it was the family's fault, that child was neglected. If the child was at risk and it was nobody's fault, he or she was dependent. If the child had committed a crime, or was in danger of leading an immoral life, or wasn't attending school, he or she was delinquent. The end result of this new legislation was quite simple: No matter what the cause, no matter who was at fault, state power could be invoked to save children. In theory, the particular label that justified state intervention had no relevance to the state's mission: the objective of the juvenile court was to provide assistance to all children within its jurisdiction. The degree of state intervention lay within the discretion of the judge. Wide discretion, broad jurisdictional categories, and informal processes were of central importance in furthering the purposes of the new legislation. The broader the definitions of delinquency, dependency, and neglect, the more kids would be eligible for aid. Since no children were to be punished, there was no need to distinguish between criminal and noncriminal acts in designating a child as "delinquent." And because the court was to be guided solely by the child's best interest, formal processes of fact finding were viewed as unnecessary.

This set of assumptions has continued to inform the jurisprudence of juvenile courts through most of the 1900's. The basic nomenclature and jurisdictional rubrics of the original legislation remained almost intact during the first two-thirds of the twentieth century. Meanwhile, juvenile justice emerged as a major industry in every American state.[6]

The conceptions of family and youth that emerge from the expansive state role in child rearing deserve separate attention. The presumed governmental role in the supervision of children during the progressive era bears a striking resemblance to the allocation of power created during that period for other regulated industries. Families, like railroads, were free to pursue private motives only insofar as they adhered to public standards. For families, this meant standards of child welfare. Consumer interests, in this case those of children, were to be protected by administrative agencies operating within broad grants of discretionary power. But three instances where the analogy between railroad regulation and family regulation might break down also prove instructive.

First, the discretion of most regulatory agencies was far more structured and regularized than that exercised by teachers, principals, juvenile court judges, and probation officers. Except in the schools, there was little rule-making. There were very few rules of general applicability in the juvenile court; individualized justice meant individualized decisions.

Second, it was assumed that the state was taking power from the corporate world when it regulated railroads. The redistribution of power envisioned by the authors of family regulation was more complicated. In matters such as compulsory education, power was taken from both parent and child. Broad definitions of neglect were chiefly a reallocation from family decision-making to public standards. Regulation of adolescents "beyond control" came principally at the expense of the child who could previously vote with his or her feet. State power to treat "ungovernable children" thus enhanced parental power: it added a powerful "or else" to the phrase "you had better behave."[7]

Third, in the case of education, the proper analogy is state enterprise rather than regulation. In the progressive view, family choice was to play a minimal role in primary education. The government's near monopoly of institutions of education was viewed as a positive—not merely necessary—aspect of child welfare. Thus, the ideology of public education was that of special-case socialism at a time when socialism was a dirty word. And it was a rather authoritarian socialism at that, particularly with regard to the children it was to serve.[8]

The Jurisprudence of Juvenility

The image of the adolescent in public law was one of absolute dependency. This was the case, for "unemancipated" minors, in a great variety of settings. It is most obvious in the jurisprudence of the new court for children.

In Professor Burt's phrase, the court was pursuing rights *for* children, intervening whether or not the particular minor wanted help, if that minor needed help.[9] In pursuing rights for children, the juvenile court was to do what was best for the child with or without his consent. To honor the rights *of* the child, by contrast, would have meant allowing a minor's will to prevail over the opinions of others in determining where his or her own best interests might lie.

In choosing between the child's will and his welfare, the philosophy of the juvenile court was unam-

biguous and consistent. The "minor" who was the subject of the juvenile court's concern was immature and
thus in need of coercive guidance for his or her best
interest. Delivering "care, custody and supervision,"
after all, requires a hell of a lot of power. The child's
immaturity was viewed as outweighing crime control
considerations in determining appropriate responses to
young persons who violated the law, at least in theory.

The same image of immaturity and need for supervision justified the age-specific prohibitions and
duties that were later to be labeled "status offenses."
Minors could not drink, smoke, wilfully absent themselves from school or stay out late, since they were regarded as too young to exercise appropriate judgments
in these matters. The young could not disobey their
parents, educators, or the court, because such disobedi-
ence would put the child's welfare at risk. In the mind-
set of the original reformers, the right to custody was
the central factor in control of child welfare; the custodial agent was expected to subordinate the minor's
wants to the minor's needs.

Much has been written about the motives of those
who were responsible for this dependent image of
youth, and about the institutions and constraints this
philosophy justified. It has been noted that the values of
the "child saving" movement were based on middle-
class images of youth that "denied... [young people]
the option of withdrawing from or changing the institutions that governed their lives."[10] And there is ample
evidence that expansive state power was used to pursue
punitive as well as protective agendas from the earliest
days of juvenile courts and extended compulsory
schooling. Child labor laws were early conceived of as

ways to protect not only children, but also adult jobs and wages.

But it is a flight of fancy to view the progressive era child-savers as part of an anti-youth cabal. Many of the key figures of child welfare and juvenile court movements were sincerely dedicated to youth welfare. It is difficult, even with the hindsight provided by history, to fault the motives of Jane Addams, a prominent advocate of the new court. And while his attitude toward youth might be called "middle class," Denver's Judge Ben Lindsey, the "Johnny Appleseed" of the juvenile court movement, was in reality a muckraking champion of the poor and the working class throughout the period he served as supersalesman for the children's court. Early in the century he became the eighth-most-admired man in America—a distinction as yet unequalled by any other member of the juvenile judiciary. He preached the virtues of community treatment, probation, and a juvenile court fueled by optimistic compassion.[11]

The Annual Report of Judge Lindsey's court contains compelling evidence of people caring about children. At least that is my reading of Table 3-1.

Thus, evidence of early twentieth century romantic and authoritarian images of youth should not be taken at face value by the historian or the law reformer. In fact, early reformers were not unmindful of the values of youth autonomy. Many of those who sought the establishment of juvenile courts, compulsory public education, and child labor laws did use the rhetoric of helplessness and dependency in arguing for an awakened public conscience and increased public investment in youth services. But many of the same reformer-

TABLE 3-1.
LOVING THE AMERICAN DELINQUENT: FROM
THE REPORT OF THE DENVER JUVENILE COURT, 1903

Facts and Figures

1903	Boys	Girls	Total
Number of reports from probationers received from school teachers during the year			2,275
Total reports received (Each report represents a personal interview between the Judge of the Court and probationer)			3,139
Baths given probationers during the year			1,150
Positions secured during the year			252
Boys sent to the beet fields for the summer			77
Needy children relieved			175
Number of garments supplied (second hand)			175
Number of garments supplied (new)			220
Total garments supplied			395

professionals recognized the value of self-reliance in adolescents and of the exercise of independent judgment when dealing with kids.[12]

The darker side of this gap between rhetoric and reality concerned the treatment of 14-year-old armed robbers and twice-convicted burglars. Writing in 1909, Judge Julian Mack declared that the purpose of the juvenile court was ". . . not so much to punish as to reform, not to degrade but to uplift, not to crush but to develop, not to make him a criminal but a worthy citizen."[13] But two years earlier, the annual report of Judge Mack's Juvenile Court reminded us, "All right-minded people are willing to have boys and girls have chances to do the right thing, but after they persistently throw chances away the same people would have a right to insist that these young people be really controlled, even if it takes the criminal court process to do it."[14] Judge Lindsey struck a more authentic chord in drafting legislation providing that "as far as practicable any delinquent child should be treated, not as a criminal, but as misdirected and misguided and needing aid, encouragement, and help and assistance."[15]

What Lindsey had in mind from the start was the protection of youth "as far as practicable." In the case of young burglars, we have spent decades, and will doubtless spend decades more, discussing just how far that is.

There is one further factor indispensable to understanding what I have called the jurisprudence of juvenility. The "boys and girls" who were the objects of public education and juvenile court control near the beginning of this century were younger than the current clientele of these institutions. Compulsory education spanned, at its inception, only the primary school years. High

school graduation was a mark of distinction. The jurisdiction of Judge Lindsey's Juvenile Court ended at the
sixteenth birthday, and the peak age for delinquency
referral in Denver in 1903 was 12.[16]

By the time the revolution in juvenile justice was
launched, we were living in a world where almost
everyone went to high school, and the juvenile court's
delinquency jurisdiction had been elevated in the majority of American states to the eighteenth birthday.

Just Before the "Revolution"

The most amazing feature of the dependent legal
theory of youth was not so much its early twentieth
century innocence as its capacity to persist unmolested
in the face of rapid social and political change. What I
have called the jurisprudence of juvenility was not
merely a quaint feature of the early 1900's; it was the
dominant legal conception of the teen years well into
the 1960's. The social dimensions of adolescence changed
dramatically through the first six decades of this century,
but the legal image of growing up in the years just pre-
ceding adulthood remained static. Most of the distinctive
features of modern adolescence developed without any
major change in legal theory.

Consider a short list of some social changes during
this period of legal immobility:

High School and College

At the turn of the century, fewer than one out of
twelve males would graduate from high school and less
than 5 percent of the population between 18 and 21
attended college. By 1960 well over 60 percent of all

American teenagers graduated from high school, more than half continued education at the college level, and 41 percent of the population between 18 and 21 were still pursuing some form of higher education by 1965.[17]

The social and economic impact of this shift cannot be overstated. In post-midcentury society, a high school diploma was a minimum condition for respectable entry into the work force. The high school "dropout" in metropolitan areas was marked with a social stigma only slightly less onerous than that associated with a criminal record. And high school was more than a credential; it was thousands of hours spent away from home or work in the age segregated institution that spawned the "adolescent society."[18] The social demand for high school and college training also lengthened the period of economic dependency for those who in earlier years would have already entered the world of work.

Urbanization

In 1900, three-quarters of our population under 20 lived in rural areas, or towns under 25,000. The pace of urbanization was swift as the century progressed, as shown in Figure 3-1.

Where kids grow up has a substantial impact on how they grow up and what kinds of adults they aspire to become. In the decades after 1920, dramatic migration occurred in the United States, as a predominantly rural and small-town populace shifted to cities and suburbs of metropolitan areas.

The "Family" Car and the "Family" Telephone

The telephone and the automobile were turn-of-the-century luxuries. By the late 1920's, both were

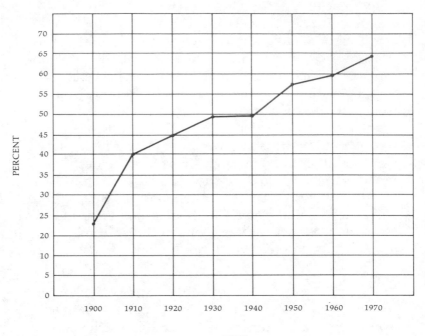

Figure 3-1   Percent of Population Under 20 Living in Urban Areas, 1900–1975

Source: U.S. Bureau of the Census, *Decennial Census Reports*, from 1900 to 1970.

transforming the character of American middle-class life, including the life pattern of the middle-class teenager. [19] By 1960, the "average" American family couldn't *be* average without one or more telephones and one or more cars. Figure 3-2 tells the statistical story.

As the 1950's ended there were four telephones

Figure 3-2   Motor Vehicles and Telephones per 1000 people, 1900–1975

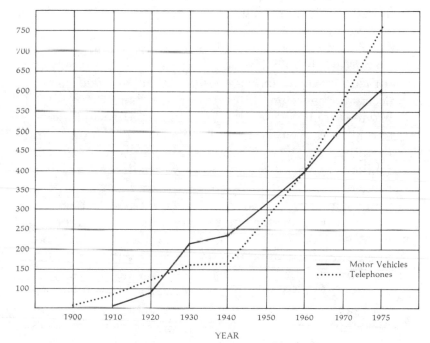

SOURCE: For Motor Vehicles; U.S. Bureau of Highways, *Highway Statistics–1975* (1977) and U.S. Bureau of the Census, *Historical Statistics of the United States, Colonial Times to 1970, and Statistical Abstract of the United States 1976.* For telephones, U.S. Bureau of the Census, *op. cit.*

and four cars for every ten people in the United States, more than one per household. Well before this point, telephones and cars had become standard accessories to the American teen years, each important and together overpowering. The family telephone provides a means of leaving home while staying put, a method of reaching the outside world that favors communication outside the nuclear family to the detriment of communication within the family.

But the telephone had a relatively weak influence on adolescent development compared to the family car (or cars) and the teenage culture that revolved around access to the automobile. A car is not merely a means of leaving home; it *is* a mobile home for the kid lucky enough to have one, or to have a friend with one. And "four cars for every ten people" suggests a nation with millions of lucky kids. The availability of cars rearranged adolescent life patterns in ways that had profound impact on parental control over teenage behavior. Consider, for one example, the consequences in metropolitan areas of shifting the arena of sexual experiment from the front parlor to the back seat of Dad's car!

For present purposes it will not be necessary to discuss the additional impact of two World Wars, radio, television, enormous growth in median family income, residential mobility, suburban development, the New Deal, the changing role of women, the baby boom, or the atomic age. By the mid-1950's all of these and more had contributed to what sociologists were calling "the adolescent society." This was and is a social order in which kids look to other kids as much as to their parents for habits, values, and aspirations. It is a form of social organization in which 90 percent of urban high school boys interviewed in one study did not want to have the same kind of job that Dad held.[20]

And all of these changes took place *before* the legal changes that are the subject of this book. While the legal theory of youthful dependency stood still, the essential elements of modern adolescence fell into place: prolonged economic dependence, age segregation, and tremendous physical mobility. In the period after World War II, the terms "teenager" and "peer group" entered our language to stay. The mixture of power and dependence that is the essence of semi-autonomy had become a fixture of American society by midcentury. Family controls had weakened to the point where a whole generation of kids could run away from home without packing a suitcase.

How such momentous change could leave the essential legal conception of youth untouched is a puzzle I will not attempt to resolve. The central point of my argument from history is this: the legal changes we will study were reactions to changes in social reality that had been in process for some time. Often there is a tendency to regard rapid legal changes as attempts by courts and legislatures to play leadership roles in reshaping the social order. In this instance it is more accurate to view the last fifteen years as a period in which the law attempted to catch up with the world, to fashion solutions for problems that had grown out of a half-century of social change.

But what's wrong with paternalism? Why shouldn't teachers be able to order kids to get haircuts? When all else fails, isn't it proper to lock up a 15-year-old who refuses to go to school? The following chapters attempt to provide a contemporary explanation of how we have come to appreciate the values of liberty and the limits of bureaucratic paternalism.

Notes

1. Juvenile Justice and Delinquency Prevention Act of 1974. 42 U.S.C. §3723(10)(H) (1974).

2. *See* Sanford Fox, "Juvenile Justice Reform: An Historical Perspective," 22 *Stanford Law Review* (1970):1187–1239; Douglas Rendleman, "Parens Patriae: From Chancery to the Juvenile Court," 23 *South Carolina Law Review* 205–59 (1971); and Neil Cogan, "Juvenile Law, Before and After the Entrance of 'Parens Patriae," 22 *South Carolina Law Review* 147–81 (1970).

3. *Youth: Transition to Adulthood*, Report of the Panel on Youth of the President's Science Advisory Committee, (1973) (hereafter Panel on Youth) at 26.

4. Panel on Youth, *supra* note 3, at 26; and U.S. Bureau of the Census, *Historical Statistics of the United States—Colonial Times to 1970* (1975) at 379.

5. Illinois Juvenile Court Act, §21 [1899] Illinois Laws 137.

6. *See* Department of Justice, Law Enforcement Assistance Administration, National Criminal Justice Information and Statistics Service, *Children in Custody: Advance Report on the Juvenile Detention and Correctional Facility Census of 1974* (1977).

7. *See* Stephen L. Schlossman, *Love and the American Delinquent: The Theory and Practice of "Progressive" Juvenile Justice, 1825–1920* (Chicago: University of Chicago Press, 1977).

8. John H. Ralph and Richard Rubinson, "Immigration and the Expansion of Schooling in the United States, 1890–1970," 45 *American Sociological Review* 943–54 (1980);

Samuel Bowles and Herbert Gintis, *Schooling in Capitalist America* (New York: Basic Books, 1976); and bibliographies therein.

9. Robert A. Burt, "Developing Constitutional Rights of, in, and for Children," in *Pursuing Justice for the Child*, Margaret K. Rosenheim, ed. (Chicago: University of Chicago Press, 1976) at 225–45.

10. Anthony M. Platt, *The Child Savers: The Invention of Delinquency* (Chicago: University of Chicago Press, 1969) at 100.

11. Charles Larsen, *The Good Fight. The Life and Times of Ben B. Lindsey* (Chicago: Quadrangle Books, 1972) at 7.

12. Larsen, *The Good Fight, supra* note 11, especially chapters 2–4.

13. Judge Julian Mack, "The Juvenile Court," 23 *Harvard Law Review* (1909) at 107.

14. Juvenile Court of Cook County, *Annual Report* (1907) at 123.

15. Larsen, *The Good Fight, supra* note 11, at 34, quoting from Ben B. Lindsey, *The Juvenile Court Laws of the State of Colorado as in Force and as Proposed and Their Purpose Explained* (1905).

16. Denver Juvenile Court, *Annual Report* (1903) at 151. The peak age of referral may have been 14, rather than 12, because of internal inconsistency in the addition of one column. But from other Tables in the Report (at 150) it seems most likely that 12 is the correct age.

17. *See* U.S. Bureau of the Census, *Historical Statistics of the U.S.—Colonial Times to 1970* (1975); and Panel on Youth, *supra* note 3, at 76.

18. For a discussion of the phrase "adolescent society" see Chapter One of James Coleman, *The Adolescent Society: The Social Life of the Teenager and Its Impact on Education* (New York: Free Press of Glencoe, 1961).

19. In the mid-1920s, for example, there were approximately

two cars for every three families in the Lynd's Middletown. Even then the right to use the family car was regarded by adolescents as a major source of disagreements with parents. Adults saw the automobile as a contribution to adolescent independence, juvenile delinquency, sexual promiscuity, and religious decline in the community. *See* Robert S. Lynd and Helen M. Lynd, *Middletown: A Study in American Culture* (New York: Harcourt, Brace & World, 1929) at 251–63.

20. James Coleman, *The Adolescent Society, supra* note 18, at 7.

Part II:

Deregulating
Adolescence

"Deregulating adolescence" is not a wholly whimsical title. I find the metaphor of deregulation evocative because of my own economic biases. The contemporary movement to deregulate business enterprise selectively does not rely on the argument that markets are perfect, just as the more intelligent advocates of reform in juvenile justice do not idealize either the decision-making capabilities of 15-year-olds or the capacities and motives of their parents. Instead, both movements are grounded on notions that liberty has value and regulation carries cost.

In groping for the appropriate balance of adolescent liberty, family authority, and state power, we must make factual guesses that inform a choice between imperfect alternatives. This is also true of railroads. In each sphere, there are a number of different public policy considerations that must be weighed. With railroad regulation and juvenile justice reform one has the sense that progress does occur—but only after wasteful vacillations between extremes of social fashion and public policy.

The justifications for recent adolescent law reforms are numerous and diverse. For our purposes, they may be grouped under four main headings: The intrinsic value of freedom of

49

choice, discussed in Chapter 4; the obligation to prevent government intervention on behalf of the young from doing more harm than good, discussed in Chapter 5; the embrace of procedural due process simply because it is fair, as discussed in Chapter 6; and, this is central, the grant of liberty as an investment in development, the "learner's permit" discussed in Chapter 7.

The following chapters will argue against regarding recent changes as resulting from a single motive or perspective. Diverse motives exist for recent legal adjustments, and they must be carefully classified before we can make judgments about why *changes are made, what general theory of families or adolescents is behind a particular change, and what implications one type of change in legal status will have on other aspects of the law of growing up.*

4

The Rebuttable Presumption
of Liberty

One of the great insights of the last two decades, while painfully slow in realization, is that even imperfect beings have interests in freedom. The social value of this insight is both principled and practical. I propose to illustrate this argument with an excursion into my own parental career, to offer a rather simple criterion for applying the insight to regulation of family life, and to discuss the proper allocation of power between parent and adolescent child when this allocation is based on the belated recognition of the intrinsic positive values of freedom.

The domestic anecdote: It is 9:30 Saturday morning. The doorbell rings and one of the neighborhood youngsters asks if my 8-year-old son Daniel can come out to play. I am a parent and Daniel is a dependent child. We will assume, against the evidence, that my parental authority is absolute and well recognized. The question is, what method one should use to decide this momentous issue of child regulation. Perform an opportunity cost analysis of Daniel's Saturday morning? Provide an arbitrary answer? Or ask two questions: Does Daniel want to play? If so, is there any good reason why Daniel should not go out to play?

A cost/benefit analysis is out of the question that early Saturday morning in my family. An arbitrary decision is convenient but unjust. It is, at its essence, an abuse of parental authority because it is good for people to do as they wish unless there are sound reasons to deny them that liberty. Children are people. Frequently there will be reasons to deny them freedom because of immaturity and dependence. But unless it is an error to allow Daniel to play, the world is a better place if he does what he wants.

So far we have been examining a personal philosophy of child rearing, not a philosophy of law. But I think the incident and the method are both illustrative and evocative of what I shall call a "rebuttable presumption of liberty," in which we recognize that *government* must ask, as a precondition to assuming power over parents or children, whether there is any good reason why such power should not reside in the private sector. This concept offers a partial explanation of changes in the state role in regulating families and youth.

The rebuttable presumption of liberty is metaphoric rather than legal; I am not here attempting to amend or to invoke the federal rules of evidence. The method I advocate is useful not only to courts but also to legislators and administrative agencies, and the concept is both a lot more and a lot less than a legal basis for children's liberation.

This last point deserves particular attention. Return with me for a moment to the question of whether Daniel goes out to play that Saturday morning some years ago. Assume, again against all the evidence, that I do not act in a kind and loving manner, but instead arbitrarily inform both Daniel and his friend—"nothing doing." Can Daniel sue for this violation of parental obligation? The answer is emphatically *no*. To allow children recourse to government in such a setting is to intensify the regulatory relationship between government and family. With respect to child-parent interaction, the rebuttable presumption of liberty is a doctrine of family liberty rather than of children's liberation.

In a family, parental authority and family privacy are the most pervasive good reasons why government should not intervene. Even though increasing family authority may reduce the freedom of choice of the individual adolescent. Giving parents the power to choose schools may cause them to send their children to schools that impose more rigorous discipline than does the local public junior high school, and reducing the number of occasions when the state will limit the exercise of parental autonomy will cut back on opportunities for children as well as others to challenge the wisdom of parental control.

One example of the drift toward family liberty in modern law reform can be found in the movement to narrow the grounds on which the state is empowered to intervene coercively because a child is "neglected." The progressive-era definition of neglect was quite broad.

There were cases where agencies of government assumed power over families because it was thought the child was being indoctrinated with improper moral and political values. This is coming to be viewed as an insufficient reason for disrupting family authority, as we realize how little government knows about what is correct for particular children.

Michael Wald, a leading figure in the recent movement toward reducing state power to intervene in cases of neglect, argues for "family autonomy" in a characteristically unromantic fashion:

> A presumption in favor of family autonomy comports with our limited knowledge regarding child rearing and how to effect long-term change in a given child's development. Extensive state involvement in child rearing would require knowing not only the characteristics desired in children and adults, but also how parental behavior and home environment affect their development. No national consensus exists about what constitutes a healthy adult. Even less agreement exists on how to achieve a healthy child, however "healthy" may be defined. The few longitudinal studies that have been done all conclude that prediction of future behavior from observation of child-rearing practices is extremely difficult.[1]

Professor Wald's thesis is not the 1950's fantasy world of *Father Knows Best*. It is, instead, based on a skeptical view of the efficacy and legitimacy of public officials second-guessing parents on questions of child welfare. The chief value of presuming parental autonomy is negative:

A system based on autonomy does not require agreement about the characteristics desired in children, the proper type of home environment, or the right way to raise children. Instead, it requires agreement about some basic harms from which we wish to protect all children. Intervention can be premised on the existence of these harms without trying to regulate all aspects of child rearing. Even then, . . . it is exceedingly difficult to delineate the basic harms which clearly justify intervention. The difficulty of deciding even the basic premises warns against a policy of intervention in less basic matters."[2]

The less we think we know, the fewer the number of occasions when we will allow governmental power to displace family authority. More tentative views about when government knows best for kids and a narrowing of the grounds for determination of neglect are thus not merely consistent with the notion of a rebuttable presumption of liberty; they are illustrative.

The rebuttable presumption of liberty becomes a species of adolescent rights when child and parent are in agreement, or when the issue to be decided relates to direct governmental regulation of adolescent behavior. One example of children and parents in alliance is the case of *Tinker v. Des Moines School District*, decided by the United States Supreme Court in 1969.[3] The Tinker children were disciplined for wearing black arm bands (with full parental encouragement) in an otherwise orderly gesture against the Vietnam war. The Supreme Court ruled that such discipline was a violation of the children's rights of free expression. I do not presume to be an expert on First Amendment doctrine, but I doubt that *Tinker* supports the proposition that children have First Amendment rights of free expression that are coterminous with those of adults.

A second case, *Ginsberg v. New York*,[4] makes it clear that First Amendment rights do not hold with respect to pornographic literature. And a mild alteration of the facts in *Tinker* will lead, I suspect, to the same conclusion. Suppose the black arm bands were swastikas? Suppose the school district or the public park was heavily Jewish Skokie, Illinois. Suppose that 22-year-old Nazis do have First Amendment rights of free expression that extend to such demonstrations? Can the same be said for their 12-year-old siblings? I think not, and I suggest that *Tinker* can thus be understood as *establishing a rebuttable presumption of First Amendment liberty*, deciding on the facts of the case that the school district's asserted rationale—maintaining order in the school—was too insubstantial to rebutt the presumption of liberty that the First Amendment carries over to the young.

One further hypothetical case illustrates the differing implications of family liberty theory and unqualified juvenile rights. Suppose the parents of a 12-year-old disapprove of their child's involvement in any political demonstrations. Family liberty theory would suggest that parental power should control. True, the rights granted in *Tinker* as *individual to the child* suggest an opposite conclusion. Yet, unless we wish to consider the locking of kids in their rooms as "child neglect," the family liberty view will prevail.

In discussing the regulatory role of public schools, we come to a set of questions that can best be illuminated by shelving the familiar but freighted free speech examples and dealing with more mundane topics. I began my discussion of the presumption of liberty with the argument that family authority and parental autonomy alone suffice to keep the government's nose out of parent-child disputes in almost all cases. The question now to be discussed is whether the school system cannot invoke the same kind of Catch-22 reasoning: All schools need authority over their pupils, and almost any system of rules can be seen as an assertion of that authority. Can we then exempt school rules, or "reasonable" school rules, from a properly invoked rebuttable presumption of adolescent liberty? As a matter of constitutional law, the answer is yes. There is no reason why the Fourteenth Amendment, a notoriously blunt instrument, need be used as a basis for deciding issues relating to run-of-the-mill dress codes. There is, however, the issue of what the legislature or the school board or the principal should regard as proper policy in considering the balance between student liberty and school authority. This is a question about which reasonable people can disagree. My tentative answer to the hypothesis of unlimited school authority is "no," although I am more comfortable with that conclusion in a high school setting than in a junior high school setting. Further, my position is based on the assumption that families and their adolescent children are not free to choose the schools the children will attend.

Consider the issue of dress codes in public schools in a non-constitutional context. A semi-blanket exemption of the school would suggest that anything "reasonable" can be legislated in terms of students' dress. Rejecting this exemption makes the school board's job a more complex one. Without attempting to make a constitutional case out of the issue, I think proper decisions are made when regulations of adolescent dress at the high school level require more justification than the school's blanket need of authority. I thus live in a world where ankle-length hair can be prohibited but shoulder-length hair should be allowed. Short shorts and skirts above the knees, see-through macho shirts and displayed tattoos are unwarranted distractions from the glories of secondary education. In my universe, however, we have passed the point where compulsory neckties and uniforms are a proper part of public education.

I would come to a different conclusion if families or children were free to choose among alternative schools. In that world, the authority of the school is based on parental choice, and any reasonable regulation can be justified as an extension of parental authority.

On weekends, any public law dress code that is age-specific becomes problematic. I should say *almost* any dress code, because a law which made age distinctions with respect to public nudity would carry some intuitive appeal. But requiring skirts for females under 18 while permitting slacks for their elders seems absurd.

There are numerous examples of adolescent freedom of choice that can be justified solely with reference to the rebuttable presumption of liberty. Indeed, one would have to hold a near-totalitarian vision of society before freedom of choice in leisure time, elective courses in secondary school, and discretion in spending earned money were not common characteristics of youth.

Thus, granting privileges to adolescents based on the intrinsic value of freedom of choice is both common and intuitively appealing. There are, however, aspects of this approach often not fully understood. The first, already mentioned, is that in most cases government policy is one of non-intrusion rather than a grant of freedom of choice to the adolescent. Shoulder length hair may be acceptable to the school board, but parental authority will prevail in all but the most wildly dysfunctional families.

Second, this particular interest in liberty should not be confused with treating children like adults. It is both more liberal and more accurate to suggest that it is treating children like people.

Third, a decision about whether or not a particular choice should reside in the public sector involves highly age-, situation-, and child-specific considerations. Within adolescence, different age groupings will call for different treatment. Different settings—school versus playground—will yield different results. Further, when possible, enlightened policy might do well to provide different choices for kids who are the same age but at different levels of maturity or in different life circumstances. [5]

One advantage of delegating power to parents is that this allows for the expression of varying family values and individual needs. There may also be advantages to decentralizing *public* decisions so that proper situation-specific answers can be provided. I, for one, would be more comfortable making decisions about appropriate hair length as a principal or school board member than as a member of the State Supreme Court, let alone the United States Supreme Court. For this and other reasons, the rebuttable presumption of liberty is one of the major approaches we will be discussing that invite confusion when infused with the language of unqualified rights and the rhetoric and mechanics of constitutional law. While situations may arise where such an admixture is a necessary one, it carries substantial costs.

Notes

1. Michael S. Wald, State Intervention on Behalf of "Neglected" Children: A Search for Realistic Standards, in *Pursuing Justice for the Child,* Margaret K. Rosenheim, ed. (Chicago: University of Chicago Press, 1976) at 248.
2. Wald, State Intervention on Behalf of "Neglected" Children, *supra* note 1, at 248–49.
3. *Tinker v. Des Moines School District,* 393 U.S. 503 (1969).
4. *Ginsberg v. New York,* 390 U.S. 629 (1967).
5. *See* Chapter 10, *infra,* "The Problem of Individual Variation."

5

Doing Less Harm

The most important influence in the movement to deregulate adolescence is also the most frequently misunderstood. When Aristotle remarked that "the lesser of two evils seems in a sense to be a good,"[1] he was probably not the first person in human history to have that insight. Yet it is a lesson we must learn each generation in a variety of contexts, and the calculus for determining the lesser evil is distressingly inexact.

Americans, in particular, are temperamentally unsuited to accepting that problems do not have solutions or that solutions may carry greater costs than the problems they address. When Eric Sevareid remarked that "the chief cause of problems is solutions" he could have been writing a capsule history of twentieth century juvenile justice.

Many if not most of our strategic withdrawals from the regulation of adolescence are justified principally because the costs of regulation—in dollars, liberty, and most importantly in youth welfare—exceed their benefits. We have come to understand that government has an obligation, when it intervenes on behalf of youth welfare, to do less harm than good. But frequently we misunderstand our motives and generate confusion when state or parental power is restricted to avoid the gratuitous infliction of harm.

A "least harm" perspective might help illuminate the puzzles of *Carey v. Population Services International*.[2] I asked in Chapter 1 whether it was correct to conclude from the *Carey* decision that a 15-year-old girl has a constitutional right to vaginal foam. And I invited the reader to consider what constitutional theory of adolescence would allow the State of New York to forbid its young persons both sex and pornography but not prophylactics. The answer, if there is an answer, is that *Carey* is a classic case of deregulation—in this instance given constitutional recognition—to avoid harming kids in the name of helping them. New York can prohibit the sale of pornography to the young because immaturity is a legitimate rationale for limiting access to erotic literature. New York can pass a law against 12-year-olds having sexual intercourse because immaturity, according to a majority of the United States Supreme Court, justifies age-related prohibition of many forms of sexual expression.

But can New York enforce its prohibition of sexual expression by the young? Will the statute book prohibition of sex abolish sex under 16? Will limiting access to contraceptives successfully legislate universal teenage virginity? If not, the impact of limiting access to contraception in the name of youth welfare is fundamentally perverse. Rates of sexual activity may not be substantially affected but the risk of unwanted pregnancy and the rate of venereal disease will increase. That is precisely the kind of help that New York's sexually active minors don't need. This is why Mr. Justice Stevens compared the New York approach to legislation that would require kids to ride motorcycles without helmets. [3]

Armed with this perspective, we can return to the question of whether 15-year-olds have *rights* to vaginal foam. The sexually active 15-year-old is given access to birth control not out of recognition of his or her mature judgment. Indeed, the *less* equipped a particular individual is for the burdens of parenthood, the stronger the argument against denying access to contraception when we cannot deny access to sex. But the "right" in this case is not a right to vaginal foam. The civil right being vindicated is the right not to be gratuitously harmed. Allow me to belabor this point; it is of fundamental importance.

Consider the allocation of power among state, parent, and adolescent child in making decisions about medical care. The general rule is that parental consent is required except when the child's need for care is urgent or so extreme that parental refusal would constitute neglect. [4] The list of exceptions to this rule that have been legislated in the recent past includes contraception, venereal disease, drug abuse, alcohol abuse, and abortion. (In the State of California, plastic surgery at 15 requires parental consent, but contraception and abortion do not.) The exceptions are instructive because no one would argue that the target groups for these services are an especially mature sub-sample of American adolescents.

In dealing with such cases, the language of unqualified rights invites a form of reasoning by analogy that is particularly confusing. Many are tempted to generalize the "right" to contraceptives, treatment for venereal disease, and treatment for alcohol and drug abuse to the "right of a minor to make independent choices about medical treatment." This is a regrettable and avoidable error.

"Privacy" legislation dealing with venereal disease and drug and alcohol abuse is really state guidance of adolescents rather than any recognition of autonomy. In public policy terms, there is only one right answer to the question of whether alcoholism, drug misuse, or venereal disease should be treated rather than ignored. For similar reasons, there is only one preferred public choice when the issue is whether or not a sexually active teenager should use contraceptives.

To say that a child can have venereal disease treated without parental consent is a one-sided allocation of liberty. It in no way forecloses the power of parents or other public authorities to compel treatment, when the condition is known, even over the objection of the child. Indeed, in the case of drugs, drinking problems, and venereal disease, it is probably a misuse of the English language to describe the legislation under discussion as a restriction of parental power. The vast majority of parents whose "authority" is by-passed by these privacy statutes would support the decision to seek help, and any parent who might wish to exercise veto power in these circumstances—for reasons of shame, retribution, or a fantasy of cure without treatment—would be guilty of medical neglect in any instance where the child is willing to seek treatment. Further, even if parental power is displaced, as may be the case with "contraceptive privacy," the rebuttable presumption of family liberty is well-served by rejecting the presumption in these cases.

We begin with the easy cases: drugs, drinking, and gonorrhea. To seek parental approval for treatment of these conditions is to inform parents of underlying patterns of behavior that are not likely to inspire parental approval. Perhaps it is good for families to have dialogs about such problems. It may be an opportunity to encourage parent-child communication. But requiring parental approval for such medical procedures encourages communication at a cost. For those kids who are fearful of such "communication" (and many have good reason to be afraid), effective treatment for a threatening condition comes at a price they are unwilling to pay. If we live in a world where such a privacy statute eliminates the opportunity for six constructive parent-child communications, but cures four extra cases of gonorrhea, I will vote for the law.

Contraception is a harder case. It is also a different case. To employ a useful cliché, requiring parental consent to treatment of substance abuse is a classic example of closing the barn door after the horse is gone. In contrast, the adolescent decision to seek contraception is future-oriented. Ideally, it would precede rather than follow sexual initiation. And while this is usually not the case, it is still a time of decision-making about the future when parent-child interaction might be helpful. The claim that allowing independent access to contraceptives undermines parental authority has some authenticity. But at the price of how many pregnancies and what increment in venereal disease?

If contraception is a hard case, teen-age abortion may be an impossible problem for "cost-benefit analysis." When teen-age pregnancy occurs, it is an emergency that is biologically unpostponable. Parental consultation may carry enormous cost and the question of whether an abortion is in an adolescent girl's best interests is more properly asked of a theologian than of a parent or a juvenile court judge. The trade-off between abortion and its alternatives is so heavily weighted by the moral value attached to fetal existence that no meaningful assessment of the choice can be made without someone making a moral judgment. Requiring parental consultation may in some cases result in the adolescent girl's learning that she has parental support for alternatives she might prefer to abortion *if* she knew her parents approved. In other cases, parental rage will be added to an already formidable list of impediments pregnant teenagers face. One also wonders about the impact of parental notice on the problematic practice of "shotgun marriage."

The trade-off between privacy and parental authority in contraception and abortion illustrates all too well the themes that recur whenever we discuss how the government can best meet its obligation to do less harm than good. First, the choice typically is between the lesser of evils. Under the circumstances, we are well-advised to remember that this is a sticky area of public policy decision-making where broad principles are frequently less useful than prudence and specificity.

Second, as is often the case, one cannot decide

what side to take in this debate by declaring a bias in favor of youth welfare. There may well be kids who consult their parents because they must, and who will therefore benefit from state allocation of power to parents, either in their psycho-sexual development, their family lives, or both. This will come at the cost of pregnancy, illegitimate maternity, and venereal disease for other young people who will not, or cannot, consult their parents. It is also possible that free access to contraception (when combined with peer pressure and inept hygiene) will have detrimental effects on some young people, while preventing anxiety, disease, and premature parenthood for others.

Third, to anticipate the issues raised in the chapters to follow, it is often difficult to resolve these problems with cost/benefit analyses. This is true for two reasons. First, in making such decisions, we swim in a sea of empirical ignorance and uncertainty about the consequences of regulating youth. Second, even if we could measure the different kinds of costs and benefits involved, it would be hard to translate them into a common currency so that judgments could be made using a standard measure of utility. How many positive parent-child interactions outweigh one pregnancy? If gonorrhea increases and pregnancy decreases are we happy or sad?

But it would be unwise to dwell on my later agenda without completing an important segment of the least-harm analysis. Early in this discussion I asked whether one could generalize from the powers granted minors in these special-case categories to a more general right to medical care without parental supervision. The answer is "no," because decisions made on least-harm grounds must be terribly specific. Plastic surgery and dental repair are not freighted with the moral front-end costs that attend family consultations about venereal disease. There is no public consensus on the proper response to teenage pregnancy that parallels the consensus on teenage drug addiction. To make least-harm decisions that are anything short of absurd is to live in a world in which vasectomy and vaginal foam are not lumped together as two forms of birth control.

Thus, Shawn Bykofsky will find little comfort and less precedential value in a case like *Carey v. Population Services International* when he argues his own brief against the constitutional validity of nocturnal curfews. If *Carey* is a least-harm case, it applies to Shawn's midnight meanderings only if the curfew gratuitously inflicts more harm than good on those subject to its regulation. Curfews exist to protect the community as well as other kids. So do minimum ages for driving, drinking, and owning handguns. Curfews give power to the police, power that may be abused in the exercise of discretion to arrest or release. But they also give power to parents: an additional weapon that may be needed, particularly on a school night, when 13- and 14-year-olds might find their friends more persuasive than their parents.

The essential notion, then, that curfews are unwarranted intrusions into family liberty or adolescent freedom is one I find unappealing. It is quite another matter, however, to say it is socially proper to lock Shawn up for extended periods of time if he stays up late, disobeys his litigious mother, or sleeps through school. In the legal universe I inhabit, the state has some power to keep 12-year-olds who are unsupervised off the street at midnight. But locking them away for their own benefit is one of the demonstrated public failures of the twentieth century. Further, inflicting drastic punishments to scare other rebellious youth is manifest injustice. We have come, then, to the saga of the status offender.

The Status Offender: An American Dilemma

Earlier, I asked what's wrong with locking up a child who refuses to go to school, if all else fails? After all, the argument proceeds, we can only do this when it is in that child's best interests as determined by a juvenile court judge. The institutions that we build and staff will be dedicated to the betterment of youth, and, therefore, the program will work. Such were the assumptions about the efficacy and efficiency of coercive state power that fueled the development of parental schools and secure training facilities to hold delinquents and status offenders. Were we *ever* that naive?

Here is a dialogue, reported in the literature, between a juvenile court judge and his "status offender" client:

> A sixteen-year-old black girl appears before the avuncular judge, for a decision as to whether she may be released from the state training school to which she had been committed for 'incorrigibility' and for having run away from home a number of times. A representative of the training school urges Martha's release, commenting on how helpful and cooperative she has been. Martha's probation officer also recommends release, telling the judge that plans have been made for Martha to attend an 'alternative

school' half a day and work the other half; a job already has been found. The probation officer assures the judge that Martha and her mother have been working through the problems originally dividing them and that ongoing social work will help them complete the process. To underscore the family's stated desire to have the youngster back home, Martha's father has taken the day off from work to sit next to his wife in court.

Peering into the record, the judge responds, "Martha, I see that you are not interested in cosmetology any more; you told the court last time that you wanted to be a beautician." Furrowing his brow in puzzlement, he asks, "Aren't all girls interested in fixing their hair and looking pretty?" He tells the probation officer that if Martha returns to public school, she will no longer be able to study cosmetology. The probation officer explains again that under the proposed plan, Martha would be attending an alternative school, not the public high school, and that a job is waiting for her. "I still think you could do better," the judge tells Martha by way of response, adding that Martha is fortunate to be in a training school that offers a course in cosmetology. "Someday you will all thank me for this," he tells the weeping youngster and her parents as he announces his decision to return Martha to the training school.[5]

This exchange parallels the authoritarian paternalism of turn-of-the-century juvenile justice at its worst. Similar "conversations" emerge from the transcripts of the early years of the Milwaukee Court.[6] But Martha's encounter with "child saving" was a 1970's event. And the debate about the "least worst" approach to adolescents "beyond control" continues, with well-meaning advocates on each side.

How can the debate continue when we have evidence like the horror story of Martha's day in court? It continues, in part, because there are horror stories on both sides of the question, among them tales of young adolescents roaming the seedy streets of major urban areas, living in squalor and risking death. With this kind of problem, the American appetite for turning from debate to concrete solutions is considerable.

Further, extreme cases (and I consider Martha's case extreme) cause us to overlook the central problems of dealing with "status offenders." Martha's most evident problem is that she is before the wrong judge. The same discretion to contain or release would lead to a different conclusion before the right judge. If the problem is bad judges, why not reform the judiciary rather than the law?

One answer is that legal standards must be designed for a world that includes both good judges and bad judges. The history of juvenile justice has put us on notice of this from the beginning. During the same period in which Judge Lindsey's Denver probation staff gave kids over a thousand baths a year (and proudly reported that fact),[7] Milwaukee Juvenile Court showed a pattern of arbitrary and authoritarian rule.[8] Inevitably, broad discretion can serve authoritarian and punitive agendas as easily as more liberal visions of youth welfare.

And it is not merely the existence of bad as well as good judges that leads to concern about the discretionary power to subject young people to the coercive force of secure confinement. Institutions become bureaucratized. Enthusiasms wane. The second generation of functionaries is less exciting and less excited than the first. And those who run large custodial institutions confront tendencies toward authoritarian control that are irresistible. The training school neither trains much nor schools effectively. It never did. A child is not receiving the care it "should receive from its family" when the door to that child's room locks from the outside. John Irwin's phrase, the "state-raised youth,"[9] was intended to be understood as almost a contradiction in terms. Governments can't raise children. Bureaucracies can't love.

The contemporary effort to rethink the government's role in dealing with status offenders involves confronting two problems simultaneously: minimizing the dangers that the immature runaway or truant can inflict on him- or herself, and finding cures or palliatives that are not manifestly worse than the disease. We *should* close down big institutions, but who will pay and at what cost? We should, to use a term of art from juvenile corrections, use "non-secure settings." My own definition of a non-secure setting is one where the kid's room and the institution's front entrance both have doors that lock from the inside rather than from the outside.

It would be difficult to overstate the importance of this distinction. Kids are almost totally powerless to affect the conditions of their lives when the door locks from the outside. But these same kids can vote with their feet in non-secure settings, and the institution must accommodate their needs, as the kids see them, to keep the kids. On the other hand, it is relatively easy to run away from a non-secure shelter for runaway youth.

For some kids, home life has become genuinely intolerable. And the dangers of exercising immature judgment
on the streets of major urban areas are quite real.
Perhaps the most prudent course would be to withdraw
the use of coercive state power except in brief "crisis
intervention" situations, and to spend money at the
same time to make a wide variety of social service and
residential programs available at the election of the adolescent. But to fancy this as children's liberation, or to
presume that such policies are costless, is absurd. The
use of hard narcotics, male and female prostitution,
death, and disappearance will sometimes result.
Tragedies will unavoidably occur.

There is, however, a bright side to a public policy
that restricts coercive intervention while continuing to
acknowledge public responsibility: necessity is the
mother of invention. We can experiment with crisis intervention techniques, hot-lines to keep runaway kids
in some contact with their parents, and residential ar-
rangements that kids might find less onerous. We can
provide these services when we have to.

One does not have to be a political economist to
understand why the food is better at thriving restaurants than in prisons or college dormitories. It has to be.
The customers can vote with their feet. The question is,
who pays? Restaurants don't subsist on government
grants, but public funding is necessary for providing
humane support for adolescents at risk. Non-coercive
networks of youth services are expensive. In other contexts, Americans have shown more enthusiasm when
spending for social control than when asked to support
voluntary social services. Money to expand the capacity
of our prisons is much easier to obtain than funding to

improve prisoners' living conditions. Let us hope priorities for kids are different. Let us hope we do not pretend the problem has gone away when the coercive solution is rejected.

Earlier, I suggested that deregulation of adolescents, based on "least-harm" justifications, should not be discussed in terms of unqualified rights. It is also unfortunate when this kind of autonomy grant is used as an argument that justice requires treating young people as fully accountable for their acts. LaMar Empey paraphrases one example of such reasoning in a recent book on delinquency:

> If status offenders are different from young criminals and are simply misbehaving youngsters who should be diverted or ignored, why not get tough with the real culprits—the young criminals?[10]

This type of argument either misapprehends the reasons why we seek to keep runaways out of secure institutions or misapplies a least-harm rationale. We are not granting the 15-year-old runaway the "right" to run away. We are cutting our losses while pursuing his welfare. Least-harm justifications do not treat 15-year-olds as if they were 25 with respect to rights. This kind of shift in social policy toward the young thus carries no obligation to treat 15-year-olds as if they were 25 on issues such as coerced economic independence or full penal responsibility.

Indeed, if there is a lesson to be learned from our experience with training schools for the disobedient that carries over to legal policy toward young offenders, it is probably an argument for more leniency rather than less. What we have learned about the destructive im-

pact of state training schools on the runaway youth argues against institutionalizing his bicycle-stealing peer.
Whether this is conclusive is, of course, another matter.

Notes

1. Aristotle, "Nichomachean Ethics II," in Clarence Morris,
   The Great Legal Philosophers (Philadelphia: University of
   Pennsylvania Press, 1959) at 18.
2. 431 U.S. 678 (1976).
3. 431 U.S. 678, at 715 (1976) (Stevens, J., concurring in
   part).
4. For a discussion of minors' rights in regard to medical
   care *see* John P. Wilson, *The Rights of Adolescents in the
   Mental Health System* (Lexington, Mass.: D.C. Heath &
   Co., 1978) at 30, 123–53, and citations therein.
5. Charles E. Silberman, *Criminal Violence, Criminal Justice*
   (New York: Random House, 1978) at 316–17.
6. Stephen L. Schlossman, *Love and the American Delinquent:
   The Theory and Practice of "Progressive Juvenile Justice",
   1825–1920* (Chicago: University of Chicago Press, 1977) at
   part II.
7. Denver Juvenile Court, *Annual Report* (1903) at 153, par-
   tially reproduced in Table 3.1, Chapter 3, *infra;* Schlossman, *Love and the American Delinquent, supra* note 6.
8. Schlossman, *Love and the American Delinquent, supra* note 6.
9. John Irwin, *The Felon* (Englewood Cliffs, N.J.: Prentice-
   Hall, 1970) at 26–29. Professor Irwin's portrait of the
   "state-raised youth" is particularly graphic. His summary
   of the major themes in their lives concludes that:

   > The world view of these youths is distorted, stunted, or
   > incoherent. To a great extent, the youth prison is their
   > only world, and they think almost entirely in the

categories of this world. They tend not to be able to see beyond the walls. They do conceive of the streets, but only from the perspective of the prison. Furthermore, in prison it is a dog-eat-dog world where force or threat of force prevails. If one is willing to fight, to resort to assault with weapons (or if he has many friends who will do so), he succeeds in this world.

Other than this, the world is made up of people with power—people who run the prison systems and enforce the rules or the people behind them who are being protected by the police, but little is known about how this works except that there is probably little chance of "beating 'em."

Irwin, *The Felon*, at 29.

10. LaMar T. Empey, *American Delinquency: Its Meaning and Construction* (Homewood, Ill.: Dorsey Press, 1978) at 583.

6

Due Process for Kids

Under our Constitution, the condition of being a boy does not justify a kangaroo court.

Justice Fortas, *In re Gault,*
387 U.S. 1, at 28. (1967)

I can perceive no basic constitutional differences between commitment to a [state] mental hospital and other parental decisions that result in a child's loss of liberty.

Justice Stewart (concurring)
Parham v. J.R., 442 U.S. 584
at 624 (1979).

Changes in the legal universe of adolescence have involved procedural as well as substantive matters. When read narrowly, *In re Gault,* the 1967 Supreme

Court opinion widely regarded as the Declaration of Independence of the "revolution in juvenile justice," addresses only the legal procedures constitutionally required in delinquency proceedings. More recent cases, dealing with matters such as minimum procedural requirements for suspension from public schools, and constitutional requirements (if any) for judicial hearings when parents wish to commit protesting children to state hospitals, have important implications for the legal status of American adolescents.

Procedural matters merit discussion in their own right, but it is also true that substance and procedure are deeply intertwined. The conclusions one reaches about the requirements of procedural due process depend on one's images of adolescents, families, and the public institutions they confront. How one comprehends and characterizes underlying substantive reality often determines procedural choices. I hope that the foregoing discussion of family authority and adolescent status will serve to illuminate the following sequence of cases that has left the due process bar somewhat perplexed.

The cases we will examine also suggest a sobering view of future litigation concerning legal rights of young persons. This sequence of cases begins with two decisions, in both of which the reasoning and the result were straightforward. These "easy" cases, *In re Gault* and *In re Winship*, were quickly succeeded by a series of much more problematic decisions. And it is probable that the shift from easy cases to hard ones will not be confined to the procedures applying to the young; as a distinctive legal sphere of adolescence develops, we can expect substantive questions to arise that are more complicated and more difficult to decide.

Two "Easy" Cases

To begin with *Gault:* Everyone agrees it was a leading case in juvenile justice, but to paraphrase Philip Kurland, where did it lead? The majority opinion in *Gault* legislated a constitutional code of procedure for accused delinquents that included the right to counsel, notice, hearing, and other components of Anglo-American criminal procedure. Mr. Justice Fortas, the author of the majority opinion in *Gault,* had written the classic liberal critique of juvenile justice in the mid-1960's: that it provided "neither the protection afforded to adults nor the solicitous care and regenerative treatment postulated for children."[1]

With this as foreground, Fortas' agenda in *Gault* was both realistic and romantic. He did not see accused delinquents as miniature adults nor foresee the juvenile court as a miniature criminal court. In rejecting the procedural means of the juvenile court he was not challenging its substantive ends or the idea that youth is a special and privileged period in American life. Instead, he was arguing that we could have our cake and eat it too; that procedural rights would not inhibit the child welfare mission of the juvenile court. Indeed, due process may itself be therapeutic. In his own words: "The appearance as well as the actuality of fairness, impartiality, and orderliness—in short, essentials of due process—may be a more impressive and more therapeutic attitude so far as the juvenile is concerned... nothing will require that the conception of a kindly juvenile judge be replaced by its opposite."[2] Meticulous due process and tender loving care can co-exist: This is the hallmark assumption of the "easy case."

The central question of whether adult-style procedural entitlements could inhibit the youth welfare mission of the court for children might have been raised in two cases decided within five years after Gault. In the first case, *In re Winship*,[3] a majority of the Court held that the Constitution required that the state must prove delinquency beyond a reasonable doubt, the same standard used in adult criminal proceedings. No serious discussion of how this high burden might increase the number of false negatives, by acquitting kids who are guilty and need help, is contained in the majority opinion of that court. Here is Mr. Justice Brennan:

> We conclude, as we concluded regarding the essential due process safeguard supplied in *Gault*, that the observance of the standard of proof beyond a reasonable doubt will not compel the states to abandon nor displace any of substantive benefits of the juvenile process.[4]

I submit that this assertion requires a more modest view of the benefits of coerced rehabilitation than earlier theories of juvenile justice contained. In criminal cases, it is an article of faith that it is better to have ten guilty men go free than for one innocent man to be convicted. This maxim supports a very high standard for proving guilt. But if the mission of the juvenile court is to help delinquents, is it better that ten kids who need help are rejected by the system than that one kid who doesn't need help receives "care and custody"? Acquitting a large number of delinquents is not a high price to pay only if we live in a world where convicting them is not in their own best interests.

Three Hard Cases

McKeiver v. Pennsylvania,[5] the 1971 decision denying accused delinquents constitutional rights to jury
trial was also the first majority opinion in the United
States Supreme Court to express any doubt about a
one-to-one correlation between full procedure and
youth welfare. Mr. Justice Blackmun, writing for the
majority, saw the possibility at least that" ... the Jury
trial as required as a matter of constitutional precept
will remake the juvenile proceeding into a fully ad-
versary process and will put in effect an end to what
has been the idealistic prospect of an intimate, informal,
protective proceeding."[6]

Why this sudden concern? It is important to com-
prehend why *Gault* and *Winship* were regarded as easy
cases by the authors of their majority opinions so that
we can understand how later procedural cases are more
complicated, more divisive for the Court, and less obviously linked to the mainstream of due process analysis.
First, *Gault* and *Winship* consider courtroom procedure
and police behavior. The analogy between delinquency
and criminal case processing is compelling both at the
police station and the courthouse. Further, the police-
man and the judge are being asked to perform acts
clearly within their competence, for the skills that attend procedural regularity are those that policemen and
judges have acquired.

Second, two issues that perplex us in other cases,
adolescent competence and parental authority, do not
arise in cases like *Gault, Winship,* and *McKeiver.* Procedural guarantees are extended in the name of fairness

rather than of adolescent autonomy. As Professor Letwin has commented ". . . the *capacity* of children has nothing to do with their right to be treated fairly, decently and humanely by their government. They are entitled to such treatment not because they are competent but because they are persons."[7]

The question of adolescent competence does arise with respect to rights to independent representation and judicial hearings *if* parent and child are in conflict about the decision at issue. In delinquency proceedings, however, the Supreme Court has assumed no such conflict exists and that both child and parent desire the minimum possible state intrusion as a consequence of the delinquency proceeding. One wonders what would have happened if Gerald Gault had been accused by his parents of being "beyond control" rather than arrested for making a dirty phone call.

What, then, makes the difficult cases difficult? We begin with the curiously unsatisfactory quality of the majority opinion in *McKeiver v. Pennsylvania*. Unless one views the right to jury trial as trivial, the strength of the analogy between criminal and juvenile proceedings would suggest a right to jury trial, particularly when charges might lead to long confinement. If, however, the institutional changes accompanying such an entitlement become a real threat to youth welfare, life gets more complicated. The case can be made that requiring jury trial entitlements in delinquency proceedings would lead to escalating penalty structures, plea bargaining, and extortion in juvenile justice because the system would have to be restructured to guarantee that less than 1 percent of the over one million delinquency referrals per year actually resulted in jury trial.[8] These adjustments would recreate the shabby realities of adult criminal justice without providing the benefits of jury trial to the accused delinquent. The case *can* be made, but it was not made in the majority opinion of *McKeiver*. A systemic analysis of the impact of jury trial guarantees was not attempted. Thus, we cannot know whether the case was wrongly decided, but we can suspect that it was inadequately reasoned.

Goss v. Lopez, [9] decided by the Court in January of 1975, was viewed as no easy case. In a bitterly contested decision, the Court held, five to four, that the due process clause requires notice of the charges against a student and the opportunity for "some kind of a hearing" as a precondition to short suspension from public schools. [10] What made the decision difficult for the Court was its institutional setting. Police are in the fair notice business, and any judge, even a judge sitting in a court for children, should know his procedural P's and Q's. But even though the consequences of school suspension are not trivial, there are substantial costs—probably including youth welfare costs—in creating a situation where the boys' vice principal must have a law degree to do his job. Imposing a constitutional requirement of formal hearing, proof beyond a reasonable doubt, or a student's right to counsel would tax the resources of the school system enormously or lead to the abandonment of suspension as a disciplinary device. Failure to recognize any right of the student to be heard would hardly comport with the values of "the image of fairness" extolled such a short time before by Justice Fortas in *Gault*. The *Goss* majority compromised by holding that an opportunity to be heard was required by the Constitution, but explicitly approving a rather low-budget hearing indeed: The vice principal need only provide the student with notice of the alleged transgression and the opportunity for the student to tell his or her side of the story. As the court recognized, school officials are hardly impartial arbiters of disputes between teachers and students.[11] Some values of more elaborate fact finding will inevitably be lost in the short, informal exchange between an accused student and a representative of the school administration. On the other hand, this kind of "hearing" might provide for a "cooling off" period and for the chance to reconsider whether suspension is an appropriate sanction. And giving a student the chance to tell his side of the story imposes few costs. While some might regard the majority as less than generous, and others (including the dissenting justices)[12] may see *Goss* as the opening wedge for an assault on school authority, my own view is that the Court muddled through rather well to a result consistent with educational and adolescent realities.

By contrast, the jurisprudence of adolescence suffered a real setback in the case of *Parham v. J. R.*, decided four years later.[13] My concern about the majority opinion in that case relates not so much to the result on the central issue as to the constitutional method of the majority opinion. The scheme of regulation under attack was one in which adults could not be committed against their will to state mental hospitals without a full judicial hearing and independent legal representation. Children (and that meant anyone under 18) could be committed against their will without an adversarial hearing as long as "informal, traditional medical investigative techniques"[14] that would be insufficient procedural protection for unwilling adults were observed. There were other issues in the *Parham* case, such as whether state welfare agencies have the same or similar status as custodial parents, but we shall not consider them here.

To use the vocabulary of an earlier chapter, *Parham* represents a clash between the presumption of parental liberty and the individual interest of young persons in avoiding confinement. Further, the issue is not *whether* the state should intervene, but *how*. The parents request state hospitalization and the children request protection similar to that afforded adults before they can be committed to the same facilities. Mr. Justice Stewart was on the mark when he acknowledged, "this is not an easy case."[15]

Chief Justice Burger, writing for the majority, defended the scheme of regulation in the name of "broad parental authority over minor children."[16] Putting aside, for present purposes, worries about empirical sloppiness, naïveté, and over-breadth, my concerns with the *Parham* opinion are two: its failure to confront genuinely difficult issues, and its nonrecognition of a period in human development that might call for a special balance of relationships between state, parent, and child. That period is adolescence.

Parham is an extraordinarily difficult problem that the Burger opinion manages to characterize as easy. There are genuine conflicts between parental authority and adolescent autonomy that must be resolved before we can properly decide whether the Constitution requires a child to be provided with counsel to represent him at a commitment or post-commitment hearing where he will be pitted against his parents. If a judge rules that commitment is improper, it is difficult to imagine the family, reunited, walking out hand-in-hand from the courtroom into a setting of domestic tranquility. Full-scale adversarial proceedings can do real harm to families, and to children. The extraordinary burden of proof which many mental health codes now attach to involuntary civil commitment may be inappropriate when parents seek help for troubled children. The maxim that first we do no harm may not lead to obvious conclusions when desperate parents seek help and psychiatric authorities agree that commitment is appropriate.

But there *are* state mental hospitals that are dumping grounds. There *are* parents that dump children. There are children, very young and adolescent, for whom the real choice should be neither continuation in a dysfunctional family nor commitment to a state mental hospital. Private (and expensive) care may be superior to warehousing kids in public institutions. Foster care or placement with relatives might be viable alternatives. Perhaps "some kind of a hearing," somewhat more structured, is necessary in the name of fundamental fairness if a child is to be held for long periods of time in a total institutional environment against his or her will. How, after all, is this case so different from one in which Gerald Gault's parents wish him committed as "beyond control" or "treated," against his will, for running away?

The reader is also asked to consider whether the use of the terms "child," "minor," "parent," and "adult" in the above discussion and in the Court's opinion is anything other than an invitation to disaster. Why should we treat 7-year-olds and 17-year-olds as if they were alike and the alternatives to hospitalization were the same? What on earth happens on that magic birthday, the age of majority, that justifies radically different minimum guarantees of procedural regularity for involuntary civil commitment? These are questions we never reach when we speak the dichotomous language of minor and adult.

Notes

1. *Kent v. U.S.*, 383 U.S. 541, at 556 (1966) (Fortas, J., delivering the Court's opinion).
2. *In re Gault*, 387 U.S. 1, at 26–27 (1967) (Fortas, J., delivering the Opinion of the Court).
3. *In re Winship*, 397 U.S. 358 (1970).
4. *In re Winship*, 397 U.S. 358, at 367 (1970) (Brennan, J. delivering the Opinion of the Court).
5. *McKeiver v. Pennsylvania*, 403 U.S. 528 (1970).
6. *McKeiver v. Pennsylvania*, 403 U.S. 528, at 545 (1970) (Blackmun, J., delivering the Opinion of the Court).
7. Leon Letwin, After *Goss v. Lopez:* Student Status as Suspect Classification?, 29 *Stanford Law Review* 627, at 642 (1977) (emphasis in original).
8. For a fuller discussion of the concomitants and possible effects of such a restructuring, *see* Franklin E. Zimring, *Confronting Youth Crime: Report of the 20th Century Task Force on Sentencing Policy Toward Young Offenders* (New York: Holmes & Meier, 1978) at 102.
9. *Goss v. Lopez*, 419 U.S. 565 (1975).
10. *Goss v. Lopez*, 419 U.S. 565, at 565–66 (1975) (Holdings).
11. *Goss v. Lopez*, 419 U.S. 565, at 580 (1975).
12. *Goss v. Lopez*, 419 U.S. 565, at 584–600 (1975) (Powell, J.,

dissenting; joined by Burger, C. J., Blackmun, J., and Rehnquist, J.).

13. *Parham v. J. R.*, 442 U.S. 584 (1979).

14. *Parham v. J. R.*, 442 U.S., 548, at 607 (1979) (Burger, C. J., delivering the Opinion of the Court).

15. *Parham v. J. R.*, 442 U.S. 548, at 624 (1979) (Stewart, J., concurring in judgment).

16. *Parham v. J. R.*, 442 U.S. 548, at 602 (1979) (Burger, C. J., delivering the Opinion of the Court).

7

Adolescence as a Learner's Permit

Here are a few of the things we cannot learn to do well without practice: making decisions, making love, driving, flying, practicing law, parenting, taking risks, saying no, and—most important—choosing the path of our lives in a free society.

Being mature takes practice. To know this is to suppose still another justification for extending privileges in public law and family life to those who have not yet reached full maturity. We gamble when we extend choices to the not-yet-adult. If we win, the experience gained in decision-making becomes an integral part of a process of achieving adulthood. If we lose, harm can come to the adolescent and the community. But in positing contemporary adolescence as a "learner's permit" period of life, we can learn much about the dimensions of public policy that this kind of gambling requires.

Choice, Change, and Adolescent Liberty

In all societies, many of the skills of adulthood can best be achieved by adults training the young. In traditional societies, the skills, rituals, and roles are passed on from the adult to the child in family, clan, or tribal settings. If the skills and social meanings of adulthood are uniform and stable, the entire transition to adulthood can be programmed by an adult society in an orderly fashion.[1] The Amish farmer trains his children and all is well, as long as the children remain on the farm. This is particularly the case when there is consensus about what types of adults individual children should become. If every boy wants to be "just like dad" and every girl the spitting image of her mother, adult roles can be taught at low tuition, beginning at an early age. If nine out of ten kids don't wish to be "just like" their parents life gets more complicated.

Today's high specialization and rapid change make training the young a more difficult and more specialized task.[2] The skills of one generation are generally not those that will be required of the next. But the larger society can provide more centralized training for social change, particularly if the nature of the change in adult roles can be anticipated. If parents are "inappropriate role models," other adults can be used to program the young for a very different future. This strategy was part of the agenda of the compulsory public high school movement during the Progressive era.[3] More recently, societies with less respect for individual liberty than ours have performed more radical experiments in training for change.[4]

But how do we train young people to be *free*? If the exercise of independent choice is an essential element of maturity, part of the process of becoming mature is learning to make independent decisions. This type of liberty cannot be taught; it can only be learned. And learning to make independent judgments is inevitably a risky process for the pupil and the larger society.

As in any gambling enterprise, we wish to maximize our gains and keep our losses small. The stakes are high.

And the calculus for determining "gains" and "losses" is somewhat more complicated than cursory inspection would suggest. In blackjack, an ideal "career" is never to lose a hand. In the game of learning to make free choices, winning every hand is poor preparation for the modern world, just as winning every hand is a terrible way to learn to play blackjack. We want adolescents to make mistakes, but we hope they make the right kinds of mistakes. An unsuccessful date may teach our child important lessons about his or her relations with the opposite sex at a far lower cost than an unsuccessful marriage.

An important part of cutting our losses during this period of development is minimizing the harm young persons do themselves, and keeping to a minimum the harm we inflict on them when they have abused opportunities in ways that harm the community. Above almost all else, we seek a legal policy that preserves the life chances for those who make serious mistakes, as well as preserving choices for their more fortunate (and more virtuous) contemporaries.

This learner's permit perspective is a splendid illustration of the limits of law as an instrument of social change. Nothing I have said has addressed the question of *when* our children should grow up. That is a question, hotly contested by theoreticians, which is in an important sense beyond the control of the state legislature. At present, we endure enormous social costs because so much "learning by experience" is centered in adolescence.[5] Some take this as evidence that youth is wasted on the young and learning experiences should be postponed.[6] Others preach that the best way of dispersing the process of learning by experience is to teach some of life's lessons earlier.[7] These two perspectives may in fact be consistent rather than contradictory. Some learning might occur earlier in a social universe that would also postpone certain more permanent decisions until later in life.

But one cannot legislate maturity. And our opportunities to control legally when children begin to "commit experience" are extremely limited in the short run by the values of adult freedom and liberal western democracy. The previous discussion demonstrated that least harm reforms kept confronting those limits in areas such as the regulation of status offenders, and New York's quixotic crusade to render 15-year-olds celibate. Peer orientation, foolhardy attitudes toward risk, and the powerful combination of social immaturity and physical mobility make middle adolescence into a mine field. But the costs of attempting to defer learning periods beyond these years are also substantial, and just because many of the negative characteristics of adolescence are, in Arlene Skolnick's words, "merely social" does not make them all that susceptible to legal control.[8]

To ask how old is old enough to date or to drive is, in this view, to ask the wrong questions. Instead, we must ask how old is old enough to learn to drive; to start a process, such as dating, that ends at competence if we're lucky; to invest, taking transitional risks, hoping that the result will be the right kind of adult.

This perspective provides general guidance on the goals pursued by legal policy toward youth, but no precise prescriptions for how these goals can be translated into effective programs or what price the general public should be willing to pay in the name of youth welfare. We want kids to participate in decisions about their education, but not at the price of sacrificing long term opportunities to avoid short term burdens. Work experience in younger years is a valuable preparation for later work, but unskilled labor should not be permitted to shut out educational experience that provides basic skills and the opportunity for later mobility. Part-time work at the local fast food emporium is valuable experience, but a lifetime behind the french-fry counter is too high a price to pay for teenage freedom of choice. Similarly, we want to give young law violators the chance to survive our legal system with their life opportunities still intact, but at what price and for how long? At the tactical level, the implications of a learner's permit perspective are distressingly inexact.

There is one issue, however, where this conception of adolescent development has decisive impact: the relationship between liberty and responsibility during the growing years. This can best be illustrated by analyzing the argument of Richard Kuh, objecting to a series of recommendations for sentencing young offenders:

> In its consideration of 'youth crime' the task force construes the word 'youth' very broadly. Were the term applied solely to those who I have heretofore regarded as juveniles—youngsters who have not reached puberty or those who have obtained it within three or four years—I would have no problems with such a lenient approach. But the task force has applied the term to individuals as old as twenty.[9]

Mr. Kuh wants to be lenient with youngsters for three or four years past puberty but no later. Why?

> The fact that eighteen-year-olds today can vote and those between eighteen and twenty-one both typically are working or able to work or completing college, are sexually and physically mature (and mentally as close to being mature as they ever will be), and are in many cases married or the equivalent.[10]

The distinguished former district attorney of Manhattan is making one of two arguments. Either he is arguing that kids are fully mature by the time they reach their eighteenth birthday or he is proposing that those given rights and privileges should as a matter of *quid pro quo* pay the full price when they violate the law. To see adolescence as a learner's permit is to reject both the evidence and the analysis he provides.

First the evidence. Are kids fully mature at eighteen because they can vote, even if they don't vote? Is that why we passed the Twenty-sixth Amendment? Kids are "mentally as close to being mature as they will ever be."

But doesn't it take more than an I.Q. to make decisions? Kids are married or "the equivalent." From the data we reviewed in Chapter 2, heaven help them. Eighteen-year-olds go to college and work, at least those lucky enough to find jobs or to finance an education. But, in my view, all of this is evidence that 18-year-olds are in the *process* of becoming adult. For that reason, using this kind of evidence to "prove" adulthood is like assuming a flight is over the moment the plane has left the ground. To impose full responsibility because adolescents have begun to make life choices is much like expecting every new bride to be an instant Betty Crocker. It is'nt realistic and it isn't fair.

In Rights Begin Responsibilities?

But what about the *quid pro quo* argument: Since they can vote they should pay the full price for committing transgressions. At the outset, we must recall the special danger of this kind of argument when dealing with "least harm" reforms. We should never use the constitutional right to vaginal foam as the basis for making any kind of judgment about the penal responsibility of 14-year-olds.

Many adolescents are working or going to college or exercising their voting rights while they are in transition to full adulthood—while they are using their learner's permit. What sentence *is* appropriate for a 17-year-old burglar if his 25-year-old brother would receive one year in prison for the same offense? Equal treatment for wrong-doing seems inappropriate to the transitional status of the learner. Of course, no learning role is complete without, in some measure, learning responsibility for conduct. Thus, part of the initiation into the adult role is building toward adult responsibilities. Just as the learning theory of adolescence implies a transition toward adulthood, so too it also implies a progression toward adult levels of responsibility. The adolescent must be protected from the full burden of adult responsibilities, but pushed along by degrees toward the moral and legal accountability that we consider appropriate to adulthood. A legal conception of adolescence compatible with this goal is discussed in the next section. Some of the problems associated with pursuing this vision are examined in Part IV.

Notes

1. The classic anthropological treatment of this subject is Margaret Mead, *Coming of Age in Samoa* (New York: William Morrow & Co., 1928); *see also* Margaret Mead, *Growing Up in New Guinea* (New York: William Morrow & Co., 1930); John Whiting, *Becoming a Kwoma* (New Haven: Yale University Press, 1941); *Childhood in Contemporary Culture*, Margaret Mead and Martha Wolfenstein, eds. (Chicago: University of Chicago Press, 1955); William N. Stephens, *The Family in Cross-Cultural Perspective* (New York: Holt, Rinehart & Winston, 1963); and Margaret Mead, *Culture and Commitment* (New York: Columbia University Press, 2d edition, 1978).

2. Anthropologists have studied this phenomenon in situations of rapid cultural change where role-models become much less uniform and have a wider range. *See, for example,* Melville J. Herskovits, *Acculturation: The Study of Culture Contact* (Gloucester, Mass.: P. Smith, 1958); *Perspec-*

tives on American Indian Culture Change, Edward Spicer, ed. (Chicago: University of Chicago Press, 1961); and Louise S. Spindler, *Culture Change and Modernization* (New York: Holt, Rinehart & Winston, 1977). A classic sociological account of the historical development and outcome of this process is Emile Durkheim, *The Division of Labor in Society,* George Simpson, translator (New York: Macmillan, 1933).

3. *See* Lawrence A. Cremin, *The Transformation of the School* (New York: Knopf, 1961); and Robert A. Carlson, *The Quest for Conformity: Americanization Through Education* (New York: Wiley, 1975).

4. The Chinese and Cuban experiences are two obvious examples, although even there keeping a consistent agenda has been and remains a problem. For China, *see* Hsi-en Ch'en, *The Maoist Educational Revolution* (New York: Praeger, 1974); *Childhood in China,* William Kessen, ed. (New Haven: Yale University Press, 1975); and R. F. Price, *Education in Communist China* (New York: Praeger, 2nd edition, 1979). For Cuba *see* Hugh S. Thomas, *Cuba; or Pursuit of Freedom* (London: Eyre & Spottswood, 1971); and Arthur A. Gillette, *Cuba's Educational Revolution* (London: Fabian Society, 1972).

5. *See Youth: Transition to Adulthood,* Report of the Panel on Youth of the President's Science Advisory Committee (Washington, D.C.: Government Printing Office, 1973). One should note that the use of "adolescence" was deliberately eschewed in this volume to avoid its manifold connotations.

6. Leon S. Robertson, "Patterns of Teenaged Driver Involvement in Fatal Motor Vehicle Crashes: Implications for Policy Options," *Journal of Health Politics, Policy & Law,* in press.

7. *See* Arlene Skolnick, Children's Rights, Children's Development, in *The Future of Childhood and Juvenile Justice,*

LaMar T. Empey, ed. (Charlottesville: University Press of Virginia, 1979); and F. Raymond Marks, "Detours on the Road to Maturity: A View of the Legal Conception of Growing Up and Letting Go," 39 *Law and Contemporary Problems* 78 (1975).

8. Skolnick, Children's Rights, Children's Development, *supra* note 7, at 163.

9. Richard H. Kuh, "Dissent," in Franklin E. Zimring, *Confronting Youth Crime: Report of the 20th Century Task Force on Sentencing Policy Toward Young Offenders* (New York: Holmes & Meier, 1978) at 21.

10. Kuh, "Dissent," *supra* note 9, at 21.

Part III

The Jurisprudence of Semi-Autonomy

Any interest the parent may have in the termination of the minor daughter's pregnancy is no more weighty than the right of privacy of the competent minor mature enough to have become pregnant. [*emphasis added*]

> Justice Blackmun,
> *Planned Parenthood of*
> *Central Missouri v.*
> *Danforth,* 428 U.S. 52, at 75

My attempt to make sense out of recent changes in legal policy toward the adolescent years inevitably rests on the premise that older kids are different from adults and from younger children. The previous section has attempted to make this explicit in a variety of settings:

- *Fifteen-year-olds have rights not to be denied contraceptives, but these are not the same sort of rights possessed by their parents nor are they extended for the same reasons.*
- *There is no principled reason to deny child support for education to kids who are old enough to vote even though it would be unwise (and possibly unconstitu-*

99

tional) to deny these same kids the power of self-determination in other matters.

- *Twelve-year-olds can wear black arm bands in peaceful demonstrations, but the same children cannot remain on the streets past curfew even if their parents don't object.*
- *There may be very good reasons to allow young girls to have abortions without telling their parents, but not on my list of such reasons is that the young lady was "mature enough to become pregnant."*

If kids aren't different, my approaches to such problems simply won't wash. If kids are different, the adolescent years require a separate and special set of legal concepts, a jurisprudence of semi-autonomy. That is the task of the following chapters.

The notion of semi-autonomy, of course, suggests unpredictable and messy problems a tidy legal mind would rather avoid. Legal classifications work best when people or problems can be put into sharper focus: "all this" or "all that" but never semi-anything. Chapter 8 argues, however, that a rigid boundary between childhood and adulthood is not consistent with the reality of achieving maturity: growing up is a process, not an event, a protracted process that should include the experience of some liberty and responsibility as an important part of becoming an adult.

Chapter 9 examines three key issues in the legal conception of youth: When should parental exercise of economic power be allowed to encumber adolescent liberty? Is it legitimate for the law to create special burdens during adolescence as part of the process of achieving full citizenship? Are there special situations that justify withholding liberty beyond the traditional age of majority? These issues overhang disputes that range from "deprogramming" kids in cults to the merits of compulsory national service programs.

Chapter 10 catalogues a number of different strategies for coping with the enormous variation in competence and judgment among kids of the same age. How can we guard against extending privileges to the immature without, at the same time, imposing unnecessary handicaps on thousands of young people well prepared to use mature judgment?

The moral, empirical, and political dimensions of these issues pose difficult problems. They are also inescapable elements of rational legal policy toward growing up and the "growing years," now and in the future.

8

Growing Up as a Process

If growing up is a process that should include making decisions and mistakes, the adolescent becomes a strange legal creature who can make some decisions but not others for a relatively long period of development. For the law, this is tough sledding. Legal thought is much better equipped to deal with full legal "persons" and with those who are not, than to make more subtle gradations of particular rights, privileges, or responsibilities. Unless the exercise of some liberty is an important part of preparing for full exercise of other freedoms, there is no reason why a single "age of majority" won't work. If, however, decision-making takes practice, then the right kind of growing up in the law takes place over time rather than on a particular birthday. This is the premise from which a legal notion of semi-autonomy derives. Growing up becomes a process punctuated by a series of legal "monuments" representing ages of majority for specific purposes.

The first section of this chapter argues that transforming the single passage from minor to adult into a series of specific adulthoods, achieved over a period of years, best approximates the social and psychological growing process. The second section of the chapter examines one technique—that of phases of privileges—that a process view of legal maturity would allow. The third section proposes a two-tiered age of majority in which two historically important birthdays—the eighteenth and the twenty-first—would be used in most (but not all) cases as the boundaries for different types of adulthood. In essence, most adult liberties would be achieved at 18, if not before, while the special entitlements of youth and some deferment of total responsibility would be in effect until 21.

Two preliminary points deserve mention. First, much of what I propose as a "phasing" approach to growing up is already a part of the complex of laws and other strategies regulating adolescents. The "learner's permit" theory of adolescence is derived from common regulatory schemes that have been developed to govern access to activities such as drinking or driving. If these strategies are already in common use, why make a fuss about them, and more particularly, why worry about something as fancy as a jurisprudence for issues as mundane as learner's permits for kids?

The answer to this question leads to my second preliminary observation. Common sense may have outrun legal theory. It may be important to state general principles about growing up that will dignify and define what is already common practice. A "jurisprudence" of the growing up years may be as useful in explaining what we do now, and why we do it, as it is in prescribing new approaches. This, at any rate, is my intention.

Binary Boxes, Dumb Dots, and Smart Machines

The necessary task of legal classification customarily uses what I shall call a binary box. This is a necessary but primitive tool in legal analysis. Imagine the ordinary light switch in your kitchen. It is either on or off. There is no in-between. Computer buffs might want to assign the value *zero* to the position of your light switch when it's *off*, and the value *one* to the *on* position. If we assume all systems are operating we need only look at the light bulb to know the position of the switch. One example of the binary-box thinking, central to this discussion, is the all-purpose age of majority. If you've reached it, you're an adult, and the light clicks on. If you haven't, you're a minor, or in the most primitive form of reasoning, a non-adult.

The "old" equal protection doctrine in American constitutional law included a more celebrated binary box. Students of constitutional law should be able to guess the box by the fact that I mention the "old" doctrine rather than our present morass. In the old jurisprudence, the degree of scrutiny appropriate in reviewing legal classifications depended on whether the classification itself was "suspect," or the right was "fundamental."[1] If either condition was met the "strict scrutiny" light flashed on. If not, only manifestly irrational classifications violated the Constitution.[2] This approach proved cumbersome when messy things like gender-based and age-based classifications started coming before the Court.[3]

The Court's response has been a struggle toward an "intermediate" level of scrutiny, one that bears a striking resemblance to old-fashioned substantive due process balancing, a process in which the judge's values could override legislative judgments with ease and frequency—anything the judge thought wrong was also unconstitutional.[4] This shift has kept law reviews flourishing with thundering criticism and querulous support. One complaint about the new "intermediate" equal protection test is that it is a completely undisciplined approach to decision-making. Under present use of the old binary test, once a classification is classified, in most cases we have reached the department of foregone conclusions. With only occasional exceptions, we failed to find sufficient compelling state interest for upholding a law involving suspect classification. And we used to be pretty good at finding some strain of rationality to sustain legislation when the suspect category light was out.[5] The calculus for intermediate scrutiny has so far eluded coherent expression.

Binary boxes are necessary to proper legal decision-making, but they can also impose great cost. Is our only real choice that between undisciplined balancing and foregone conclusions, in packages so large and categories so crude that the risk of injustice is great?

Permit me a digression and I'll attempt to provide an answer. One of the miracles of the modern age is that my sixth grader can spend ten dollars to get a machine that knows twenty times as much math as I do, fits in his pocket, comes up with answers as soon as the button is pushed, and can count to a hundred million. It is a very smart machine. It is a smart machine that is built with a collection of millions of very dumb dots, dots much like that light switch, that become miraculous when multiplied. Put a few dots on a little chip of silicon and watch what happens. Fifteen dots can count from zero to 32,767. One small silicon crystal can be programmed to play better chess than most Americans.

Enough metaphor. My argument is that the process of becoming adult can be comprehended by the law by using *a number of* interrelated binary-box classifications. The phases of childhood and adolescence provide one set of boxes. Decision-making contexts provide another set of boxes: living at home or on one's own, working or in school, custodial versus non-custodial parent. Over the course of adolescence, lights switch on—one, two, or ten at a time, like city lights at night. But years go by until they all light up and full adulthood in all its legal meanings has been conferred. In this kind of world, when California gives its 18-year-olds the right to vote it retains the question of appropriate maximum legal age for educational support for a separate and specific analysis.

But when should the lights go on? And in what order? What substantive principles should determine when a privilege or power of decision-making in a particular area is conferred from state to child or shifted by state law from the family to the kid? Some guidance on these matters can be obtained from previous chapters.

The rebuttable presumption of liberty, by definition, provides no public guidance for *when* during adolescence the shift from parent to child occurs. It leaves that issue in the private sector. It can help, however, to clarify the reasoning behind a public decision.

Our least-harm discussion does give guidance on appropriate ages of deregulation because it teaches a powerful lesson about the law's dependence on the world. Whenever state or parental regulation is harming more than helping, policy should probably be changed. Whether we should provide vaginal foam to 12-year-olds is a function of whether 12-year-olds are sexually at risk. But even when we do this, no "light" goes on because deregulation *in the name of least harm* is not a part of growing up in the law. The civil right not to be gratuitously harmed is one we owe to all children of all ages. The due process analysis in Chapter 6, especially my discussion of *Parham v. J.R.*, counsels that in conflicts between the adolescent and his still-custodial parent, procedural requirements may be unique.

But our hopes for a viable theory of legal adolescence rest largely on the learner's permit perspective. Here, if anywhere, lies the hope for some principle to guide the transition to legal adulthood. Strategies of phasing and differing presumptions of majority are not fancy, but I hope they make some sense.

Phasing

Some things should happen before other things, and other things shouldn't happen together. Kids should probably neck and then pet for a time before engaging in sexual intercourse, but the law can't do much about that. Families can, but not family law. Kids should have access to contraception before they are sexually active and here the law *can* help. Kids should also have access to any driver's training we want to give them before, rather than after, we extend the privilege of having a driver's license. These are areas where a phasing perspective tells us the order the law should impose or encourage.

On other occasions, we may decide that two learning periods should not begin at the same time: Sixteen may or may not be the right birthday to extend the privilege of learning to drive by doing it; sixteen may or may not be the right age to extend freedom of choice about drinking. But there is *no* right age during adolescence for doing both at the same time if, as I suspect, the risks generated by learner's mistakes are exponential when learning to drink and learning to drive are mixed.[6]

This gives me the opportunity to say something kind about Michigan and the other states that re-examined their minimum drinking ages. A "phasing" strategy can be either tidy or worldly but not both. The reasons relate to the social realities of the teen years. Put bluntly: privileges leak. When a 16-year-old boy is legally entitled to drive, his 14-year-old girlfriend will be in the passenger seat. And 47 percent of all young persons killed in automobile accidents are passengers rather than drivers, including 66 percent of all young females killed in accidents.[7] When 18-year-olds can buy beer and wine in package stores, rest assured their 16-year-old dates will also be drinking in some secluded parking area.

What I like about the Michigan and Massachusetts debates on the drinking age is that the leakage problem was recognized. What troubles me is the punitive crudity of the solution. A learner's perspective might suggest a beer age before a liquor age; or, perhaps, a distinction between on-premises drinking of beer and wine and off-premises privileges, with the latter coming later. The "on-premises" proposal gives us some control on the quantity of alcohol consumed and reduces the problem of leakage to younger adolescents. It may, however, increase driving after drinking if it displaces home consumption with tavern drinking.

All of this brings us to what is certainly one of this century's most problematic laws. Back before we all had automobiles, temperance unions lobbied to pass laws forbidding the purchase or consumption of alcoholic beverages within a one-mile radius of college campuses.[8] In a world where most folks walk, this might reduce campus consumption of alcoholic beverages by increasing somewhat the difficulty of acquisition. In a world full of cars and drivers' licenses, this means that kids will drive to and *from* their pubs and discos. In that kind of world, the best place to have a bar is next door to the dorm, if we are willing to trade increased consumption of alcohol for reductions in high-risk driving and better control of under-age drinking.

One final word on phasing: If we know that one of two privileges must be deferred for one or two years beyond the other, how should we select which comes first? In many situations, the sequence will be determined by the difference in total social cost we anticipate from the different orderings. But what if it makes no difference which comes first? Then there is only *one* right answer. Pick the one that most kids want the most. The fine irony is that this calls for an election, at least in metaphorical terms, in which only kids can vote.

Two Ages of Majority?

I have argued against using a single binary box, specifically age 18, as an all-purpose criterion for adulthood. By now, the argument has become sufficiently complicated that we can retrospectively appreciate the value of binary boxes. How shall we make our hundreds of decisions about age grading? Doing this on an *ad hoc* basis is a bit messy when any age is arbitrary. But is that our only alternative?

The age of majority in American law is associated with three different attributes of "adulthood": liberty, entitlement, and responsibility. Liberty is the right to exercise the same kind of freedom of choice, as far as the state is concerned, as other adults. One familiar example is the right to autonomy in making decisions about medical care. Entitlements are those special opportunities the state might wish to provide only to those who have not yet reached adulthood. The Job Corps or the Depression-era Civilian Conservation Corps might serve as examples. Responsibility means paying the full price for misdeeds and being responsible, as are adults, for self support. Why not make the age of majority 18 for liberty and 21 for entitlement and responsibility? The advantage of this scheme is its capacity to convey full benefits without full burdens. The disadvantage is that it is too crude and possibly too one-sided a view of the last years of adolescence.

But the scheme can be refined somewhat. With respect to liberties, why not the eighteenth birthday as a presumptive age of majority, one where we confer liberties not previously granted, unless there is a very good reason not to. Freedom of choice in medical care, for example, might not extend to the right to request and obtain vasectomy at age 19 in the name of zero population growth. In the matter of entitlements, a good argument can be made that educational and job skills entitlements should not be age-specific. But if they are, why not presume 21 as an age of majority unless there is good reason for adjusting it upward or downward?

With respect to responsibility, such as the "right" to attend college without a non-custodial parent's support, why not presume age 21 unless there are good reasons to depart from that threshold? The system is not airtight. It provides guidance rather than command. There are loopholes, but perhaps there should be loopholes.

Anyone who tries to sell presumptions must deal with the question of how strong a case against the presumptive age must be made before the presumption yields. My own view, with respect to the two-tiered age of majority, is that the presumption is a strong one. It should require something special before a privilege is withheld beyond age 18. It should require something special before responsibility is imposed or developmental entitlements withdrawn prior to age 21. In my system the two presumptions gain equal strength for different reasons. One presumption derives its strength from political as well as social considerations while the other relies on what I consider to be social fact.

The presumption of privilege has to be a strong one. The law has come too far down the road of extending privilege at the eighteenth birthday to make a general retreat. While I do not consider the Twenty-sixth Amendment to be an Equal Rights Amendment for our children, there is cost and friction in giving an 18-year-old a right and then taking it away—social cost and social friction at a time when relations between the generations are already difficult. I am not saying adjustments are out of the question, but I *am* suggesting that we should choose our ground carefully in such matters.

The presumption that full responsibility be postponed to 21 (and in some cases beyond 21) is a strong one because I simply do not believe that it is correct to speak of the average 19- or 20-year-old as fully adult in the modern world. If I'm wrong, the presumption weakens.

Treating different categories of adulthood in different ways requires us to characterize particular policies. This isn't always easy. Is a lower minimum wage for teenagers an entitlement or a burden? What about proposed programs of compulsory national service that would enroll young persons between 18 and 21?

The minimum wage proposal, as it now stands, is a hard case because the observer must decide about the economic impact of allowing kids to work at lower wages before putting a label on the policy. More kids will work, but some of them will work at lower pay than they would if a uniform minimum wage were retained. My own best guess is that in an economy suffering from high unemployment, a two-tiered minimum wage is an entitlement, giving young persons an additional edge in competing with their elders for scarce jobs. I would be more comfortable with that characterization if we were discussing a subsidized work program that gave the kids adult minimum wage compensation and paid the employer the difference. That clearly is an entitlement, and a presumptive age of 21 or higher is thus not troublesome.

One can come to the same conclusion, on somewhat shakier ground, if one truly believes a program of compulsory public service is intended as a youth welfare measure rather than as a shill for the all "volunteer" army. One method of making that belief possible would be to require one year of non-military service and to maintain the system of two-year enlistment commitments in the military services.

Under such circumstances, coerced public service becomes a collision of presumptions, for it is at one and the same time an entitlement and a restriction of liberty. In a world where most kids finish high school, the only way such a system can work is for it to start at age 18. It is there we must choose our ground carefully in restricting liberty. It would have to be a very good program indeed to justify this level of compulsion.

One final note: There is some justification for asking whether my concern over the advisability of adopting a single age of majority or multiple ages of majority isn't a trivial triumph of form over substance, typical of mediocre lawyering. Can we not achieve the same youth-protective policy by removing all the disabilities of minority at age 18, while treating issues of responsibility and entitlement as unrelated to the fact that someone who has been a "minor" has reached a particular magic birthday? Perhaps. But it may be worthwhile to discuss these matters in terms of multiple ages of majority for two reasons. First, it is not clear that removing *all* "legal disabilities" on a young person's eighteenth birthday is necessarily good public policy. Yet the gravitational force generated by using eighteen as a uniform age of majority is substantial. Experiments, such as those currently being performed in alcoholic beverage control, would be much harder to perform after a sustained period of a single majority birthday of 18.

At the same time, a single eighteenth birthday age of majority tempts the legal formalist to link responsibility and entitlement issues with questions of adolescent liberty. Conceiving of legal majority as a multiple age phenomenon may protect older adolescents from being punished in the name of liberation. Those arguing for the single age of majority frequently support their position by pointing to the adult "responsibilities" assumed by those between 18 and 21. Might they someday come to regret this linkage?

Notes

1. *See, for example,* Gerald Gunther, *Constitutional Law: Cases and Materials* (Mineola, N.Y.: Foundation Press, 1975) at 665–689; and Laurence H. Tribe, *American Constitutional Law* (Mineola, N.Y.: Foundation Press, 1978) at 991–1136.

2. Gunther, *Constitutional Law, supra* note 1, at 665–689; and Tribe, *American Constitutional Law, supra* note 1, at 994–1004.

3. *See* Laurence H. Tribe, "Childhood, Suspect Classifications, and Conclusive Presumption: Three Linked Riddles," 39(3) *Law and Contemporary Problems* 8 (Summer 1975); and Tribe, "Structural Due Process," 10 *Harvard Civil Rights—Civil Liberties Law Review* 269 (1975).

4. *See* Tribe, *American Constitutional Law, supra* note 1, at 1082–1089.

5. *See* Tribe, Childhood, *supra* note 3; Tribe, *American Con-*

stitutional Law, supra note 1, at 994–1004; and Gunther, *Constitutional Law, supra* note 1, at 665–688.

6. The peak age group for motor-vehicle accident and fatality rates is 20–24. The possibility of a lag of some years in the risks of learning to drive and in driving is thus indicated. Such a lag may possibly be tied to drinking age; although, inasmuch as the risk rates for the peak age group are not tied to miles traveled there is much controversy over their interpretation. *See Minimum-Drinking-Age Laws* Henry Wechsler, ed. (Lexington, Mass.: D.C. Heath & Co., 1980) especially Chapters 4 and 6.

7. *Vital Statistics of the United States, 1976,* volume 2, Part A, Table 4–2 (1978).

8. *See, for example,* Warren L. Johns, *Dateline Sunday, U.S.A.* (Mountain View, Ca.: Pacific Press Publishing Association, 1967); and William G. Harper, *The Texas Blue Laws* (Hicksville, N.Y.: Exposition Press, 1974).

9

Three Key Issues

Any effort to confront legal issues relating to adolescence must deal with three issues:

- How should the law deal with the economic dependence that is epidemic among younger citizens?
- Should we impose burdens as well as benefits on the transition to adulthood?
- Are there circumstances where we should postpone full adulthood beyond the twenty-first birthday?

What follows is a preliminary attempt to discuss these difficult and controversial issues.

Economic Dependence and Adolescent Liberty

We live in a world where there are families with money and families without money. In a functioning family with money, the transition from family authority to adult-style liberty may be postponed by the fact that Dad can stop writing checks if he doesn't like Junior's hair style, grade point average, or girlfriend. The ability to vote with one's feet is sharply curtailed when one is dependent on others for the money to buy shoes. Unless, of course, we pass a law that gives Junior the right to sue for "child support," and a judge the responsibility of figuring out what would be in Junior's "best interests."

We shouldn't pass that law. The rebuttable presumption of family liberty has not been defeated. The "equal protection" pitch—that other kids the same age who are on their own have rights—ignores the fact that voluntary economic dependency is itself a role that justifies the difference unless it is manifestly abused. Even then, the costs of intervention in such cases are substantial. To assume that family money should be transferred to the children is not warranted. If parents continue to have custody, their judgment, rather than state judgment, should prevail.

Living in a world with many binary boxes allows us to make fine but often important distinctions. Consider the Jones family, actually the former Jones family. Mr. Jones is both very rich and divorced. Mrs. Jones gets an awful lot of child support money. Mrs. Jones and 17-year-old Jane want Jane to go to Smith, while Mr. Jones prefers Oral Roberts. Jane can go to Smith. Mrs. Jones can sue and should win.

As soon as custody and economic support are separated, it is wise to have power reside in the custodial parent. This is for two reasons: First, there are special dangers of abuse by non-custodial parents pursuing their own economic self-interest. Second, it may be that the "family" in the phrase "family liberty" does not necessarily include a non-custodial parent. And, yes, I would agree to the same result if it were Mrs. Jones who wanted Oral Roberts *if* her daughter agreed. If Mrs. Jones and her daughter disagree on college, then a change in custody to Mr. Jones is warranted if he and his daughter agree.

Where economic support for adolescent liberty is the goal, public funds should be spent. We may want to spend that money on runaway shelters or free public universities for kids from both rich and poor families. This step will transfer power from parents to kids. But to take the additional step of taxing families, so that the level of support depends on the wealth of the family is to stack the deck against family liberty when father may well know best. Economic support within intact families should be a matter for the "private sector." This economic power is, and will remain, a major constraint on adolescent freedom of choice.

The Burden Problem

It is almost an embarrassment to have deferred discussion of questions such as the military draft and compulsory service programs to this late a point. These are, to put it mildly, "high priority" issues for adolescents. Each raises a variety of problems, and all raise what I shall call the burden problem: Is it appropriate, as a rite of passage, for the young to sacrifice, in the public interest, as a transition to achieving full citizenship? Is it appropriate to charge for a learner's permit, or for the license that full citizenship represents? If so, how much? And under what circumstances?

The worst way to begin any discussion of this issue is to mention the military draft. While the argument can be made that wars are waged because congressmen can't be drafted, our convulsive recent debate about very "selective" service has little to do with rites of passage. Rites of passage are universal; one of the stronger arguments against the draft was that selective service was indeed selective, and selective in profoundly predictable ways. Secondly, the military draft never did and never will create an all-adolescent army. Those of us who oppose the draft would not change our minds if able-bodied adolescents were excluded. Finally, paying a price for a learner's permit and getting killed in Vietnam are qualitatively rather than quantitatively different. The debate about conscription focuses precisely on that qualitative difference; it is not an analysis of the burden problem.

But the moral career of the military draft has literally screwed up discussion of the burden problem for two reasons. The first, and most obvious, reason is that conscription has been the only recent significant burden associated with adolescence. The second problem is that because the draft is profoundly controversial, and because we have turned the selective service on and off, almost any burden imposed as a rite of passage on tomorrow's adolescents will appear unfair because yesterday's adolescents got away scot-free.

But consider a plan for universal, one-year, four-dollar-an-hour public service. Assume the proposal allows the individual youth to pick any year between his or her seventeenth and twenty-second birthdays: One year of hospital service, public employment, or the like, or two years of military service, would discharge the obligation. For those who view such work as a burden, and there will be many, the plan will always seem unfair because those who have turned 22 the day before the law becomes effective have escaped. For this reason, any program of public service based solely on the needs of the nation, rather than on the needs of the young, should probably be viewed with skepticism if not rejected.

Under usual circumstances, if the nation needs public service, it should probably compel the services of a wider group of its population. But this is an historical accident. If we could start all over again, it would be appropriate to require necessary public service as a rite of passage for adolescents. The problem of inequality would be solved because everybody who lived to achieve full citizenship would have paid his or her price. There would be no older brother who had beaten the system.

And there is one burden consistently associated with adolescence in American life that is not so unfair—the burden of waiting one's turn. Consider the argument against prohibiting 18-year-olds from drinking because 16-year-olds will abuse alcohol. Is it fair? I think the answer is yes. Any system of age classifications is arbitrary, and the leakage problem is not unique: After all, there are 17-year-olds and 16-year-olds who can make responsible decisions about alcoholic beverages. The law will not allow this, but the burden is temporary and will be outgrown. This kind of burden, treating grown-up kids as if they were not, is a tax on adolescence than can be justified in many cases.

One last problem. In discussing a program of compulsory national service, I argued that such a program would be difficult to justify solely on the basis of the nation's need for public service. But what if we were to institute that very same program of national service out of the genuine belief that such service is necessary and positive training for modern citizenship? What if we really believed that, collectively, but many of our children still regarded it as a coercive burden? Would it be permissible, in that world, to legislate compensated compulsion for 18- and 19-year-old young persons? (It would have to be a particularly creative and expensive program, by the way, before I would believe that this was the true legislative intent.)

Under such circumstances, the analogy with raising the age of compulsory education in the early years of this century becomes instructive, though inconclusive. The 14-year-old whose older brother had a right to drop out of school could not complain about his extended free public education because it was in his welfare. No matter that the minor regarded it as a burden; it was his ill-educated brother who had not been served. But the analogy is incomplete: 14-year-olds were and are dependent minors. Youth welfare and educational need justifications are sufficient to defeat the rebuttable presumption of liberty unless one belongs to a well-functioning Amish community with no welfare rolls and no crime rate.

But now we are talking about 18-year-olds. What

are they? Complete citizens because they can vote? Semi-autonomous but too old to compel for their own welfare? Or semi-autonomous and not quite too old for this last stab at coercive paternalism? The jurisprudence of semi-autonomy would suggest the proper resolution of this particular coerced youth welfare burden is the difficult choice between these two visions of semi-autonomy. It will be difficult but worthwhile to strive for a legal view of late adolescence that is flexible enough for national service proposals to be judged on their merits rather than categorically excluded from serious consideration.

The Issue of Super-majority

In theory, a jurisprudence of semi-autonomy permits the deferral of liberties, entitlements, and responsibilities past the twenty-first birthday. In practice, deferring liberty might prove quite difficult. In this society, maturity and competence are probably not fully realized by age 21. In a social sense, then, perhaps we can't grow up that soon; in a legal sense, for almost all purposes, we must.

There are, however, some exceptions to this general rule. Twenty-one is not old enough to be a United States Senator and 30 is not old enough to be President. When the stakes are that high, the Constitution requires attaining an age of what I shall call super-majority before one is eligible for office.

Why not super-majority minimum ages for consumption of alcoholic beverages? If the insurance companies are to be believed, single male drivers under 25, not just under 21, are the risks.[1] Why not raise the purchase age that high? Let me try to state my case clearly. That kind of law is not merely politically implausible and socially divisive, it is also unjust. I have argued elsewhere that our current deferral of liberties can be justified because adolescence merely *seems* like forever. But using age-grading to defer common liberty into the mid-20's is exploitation in almost every case. Adding four or seven years onto an already long wait is simply too much of a burden. The twenty-first birthday has a long history of serving as the outer boundary for legal disability based on age.[2] There is no good reason to risk the legal incoherence and social division that pushing beyond this limit would impose.

The same tradition does not, at present, apply to the years between 18 and 21. This historical moment, so close to the Twenty-sixth Amendment, provides the opportunity to experiment with super-majority extensions past the eighteenth birthday, either to age 21 or to some intermediate age. As we have seen, the presumption of liberty at age 18 is a strong one. This does not mean, however, that we have passed the point where extensions within late adolescence carry the same cost as postponing legal adulthood past age 21.

All of this assumes, of course, that an individual's age should be an important element of his or her legal status. Why is that? What are the alternatives? That is the concern of the following chapter.

Notes

1. *See* Insurance Information Institute, *Insurance Facts*, annually; and National Safety Council, *Traffic Safety*, annually.

2. *See* Institute of Judicial Administration/American Bar Association, Juvenile Justice Standards Project, *Rights of Minors, Tentative Draft* (Cambridge, Mass.: Ballinger Publishing Co., 1977) at 18–19; "Legislative History of Title III of the Voting Rights Act," 8 *Harvard Journal of Legislation* 123 (1970); and *The Rights of Young People*, Alan N. Sussman, ed. (New York: Avon Books, 1977) at Appendix A.

10

The Problem of Individual Variation

A further problem haunts any jurisprudence of adolescence, one we can grapple with but never really solve. We observe it whenever we walk into an eighth-grade gym class. We confront it whenever we talk at length with a group of college freshmen. We see it in our children's lives and the lives of their friends. This is the problem of individual variation. Human beings simply don't all grow up the same way. Competencies are acquired at different levels and in different orders. Kids vary enormously.

Because this is so, a perfect fit between the realities of adolescent development and the law's response to growing up would give each individual child his own personal statute book, designed to respond to individual developmental events with precisely timed changes in legal status. This, of course, will never happen. Instead, we must choose between or mix three strategies: age-grading, individual competence testing, and decentralized discretion.

Age-grading is the tidiest, most "legal" response to the problem of individual variation. It should therefore come as no surprise that it "solves" the problem of individual variation by ignoring it. Nobody is old enough to vote at 17 and everybody is on his or her eighteenth birthday. Twelve-year-olds who read the *Political Science Quarterly* can't vote but 19-year-olds who read *Mad* magazine are enfranchised.

In sharp contrast, a pure "competence" approach would attempt to design a test of political literacy, struggle toward a rough sense of what should be a passing score, and make anybody, at any age, pass the test once as a precondition to the franchise. Smart kids could vote at 10 and some of their classmates never. Competent drivers of *any* age could get their licenses. Of course, there are problems. Do we really know how to test political competence? Do we really know how to set a passing score? Even if we could define appropriate levels of minimal competence, what is to prevent our egalitarian sympathies from pushing the passing score well below true competence? Finally, what about the stigma of not passing the test? How does the older brother feel when he flunks the test his sister passes? What about those people who will never vote?

If objective standards are difficult to create, discretion provides an alternative approach to individual variation. Since every kid is unique, have another human being examine the individual and make a decision.

Since there are millions of kids, this discretion will be decentralized. This is the least "legal" solution to the problem. It is a government of men, not laws. In its pure form, it carries unacceptable dangers of abuse.

But elements of discretion, when mixed with other mechanisms, are indispensable to a decently operating legal system. The tyranny of unguided discretion is why we have retreated from the lawlessness of the original juvenile court. The necessity of discretion is the mother of a number of legal inventions: the presumption of family liberty, the "emancipated" minor, the "special cases" exceptions to minimum ages for marriage.[1] The cost of living in a world of rules without exceptions is very high.[2]

Sometimes three wrongs can make a right. Each of the coping strategies I have described is imperfect. But systems that mix these three strategies may be less imperfect. Consider the case of driving, a privilege which is rationed by a system that uses all three strategies.

The age-grading is straightforward. My child has to be 15-and-a-half or 16 before he can get a learner's permit and 16 before he gets his license.[3] But age alone is not enough. He also has to pass a competency test. If the testing system is not corrupt, the public interest in avoiding incompetent drivers will keep the standards for driving from falling too low. But the Department of Motor Vehicles can only test driving ability, not personal judgment or the willingness to abide by the law. During adolescence, this kind of drivers' testing deals with a fraction of what it takes to be a safe driver. Age-grading and discretion are thus necessary supplements to a rational system of allocating drivers' licenses.

The discretions in the current system are many. Parental consent is frequently a legal necessity and almost always an economic precondition to teenage driving.[4] Legal requirements of liability insurance permit insurance companies as well as parents to discourage driving by setting high-risk rates.[5] The fact that human beings grade driving tests is yet another loophole, unless you truly believe that a 55-year-old widow and a 16-year-old boy will be held to identical skill standards by the fellow administering the test.

But why couldn't the system work just as well without age-grading? Pass the test, get Dad's permission, buy insurance, and drive at any age. My first problem with such a system is the added burden it would put on parents of the 14- and 15-year-old kids who would turn up the heat on Dad the minute the law was changed. Age-grading, in theory, usurps parental authority; in practice, millions of parents bless it as the good reason they need to postpone what should be postponed. Age limits help strong parents avoid saying no and protect weak parents from saying yes.

The fact that we live in a world with weak as well as strong parents suggests another reason why minimum ages make social and legal sense—the "leakage" problem. This was discussed in Chapter 8, but it bears repeating here. If I'm weak-willed and my son passes the test, your daughter will be riding in the front seat of the car. Because this is so, the minimum age for driving has yet another public purpose: It protects other peoples' children from the consequences of inappropriate parental discretion. This is not a small matter. Data on traffic deaths provide two convincing demonstrations that the hazards of driving are socially spread among adolescents. The first evidence concerns the downward spread of driving risks. For males, the peak age group of traffic fatality is 20 through 24. For females (with lower risks), the highest risk age group is 15 through 19.[6] These data, and the high proportion of girls who die as passengers, suggest that risks generated by older drivers are a major threat to younger passengers. Nor are girls the only group at risk. Of the 4,010 boys between 15 and 19 killed in traffic accidents during 1976, 1,630 (41 percent of the total) died as passengers.[7] And not even the strongest parent can guard against the possibility of his child riding in a friend's car without fantastic curtailment of the child's freedom of movement. What economists call the "externalities" of weak parental discretion in making decisions about adolescent driving are substantial indeed!

There are other ways in which youth welfare is served by waiting in line until a specific birthday for the privilege of driving. Imagine the status symbol that a driver's license would become in a world without age-grading. All 14-year-olds would envy the lucky few. The children of strong parents would look up to the children of the weak. And since we can't judge judgment, more of our kids would drive and more of our kids would die.

Further, many of our children would suffer a fate, to them, worse than death—the stigma of not driving when other kids their age are driving. They would resent the unequal treatment of 14-year-olds because *they* believe that age is important. If anything, 16 is too young to drive. If anything, further downward extensions of driving would make things worse for kids, family, and society.

Permit me one more excursion before imposing some discipline on the problem of individual variation, an excursion into the mix of strategies we use to determine what motion pictures our children can and cannot see. The current industry system for rating motion pictures is one of the most familiar and fully articulated approaches to the problem of individual difference, family choice, and age-grading. "G" pictures are made for kids, and on occasion, their parents might enjoy a "G" picture as well. But "G" ratings are the stuff of Walt Disney and Saturday matinees. A "PG" rating is the essence of family liberty theory: My child can see the film if I don't mind, whether he is 4 or 14. But if I am a conscientious parent, the parental guidance rating advises me to do some research. There is something about the film that may be inappropriate for my child. The people at the movie theatre won't stop him from seeing it, but perhaps I should.

In contrast, the "R" rating is the motion-picture equivalent of nocturnal curfew. My kids can see an "R" rated film only if I'm there too. Unlike the "PG" rating, where parental guidance is requested, the motion picture association demands my personal participation in any decision to allow my child to see the film.

The final stage in this fine-tuned regulation is the "X" rating. And here, father does not know best. If you're under 18, no movie, even if Dad says yes. Of course, particular films may be misclassified and parents may make mistakes. Movie censorship may not be appropriate for 16-year-olds. But the design of the system is an eclectic wonder.

Choosing Strategies

Are there general principles to guide us on the matter of when different strategies for coping with the problem of individual variation are appropriately used?

There are, in my view, a few such principles. Competence testing makes sense in public law when one of two conditions is met: (1) Extending a privilege creates a danger to the user and to others, or (2) A special privilege is requested—for example, entering practice as a doctor, lawyer, or accountant. Even in these circumstances, because our capacities to test competence are limited, testing alone should rarely be a sufficient condition for allowing a dangerous privilege.

Discretion, particularly parental discretion, is an important part of a well-conceived regulatory scheme unless there is a good reason to exclude it. This is why we live in a world where 15-year-olds need parental consent for plastic surgery but not for treatment of venereal disease. But parental consent is in many cases not a sufficient condition for granting liberty. The law must allow for stupid parents as well as wise ones, weak as well as strong.

Age-grading within adolescence is particularly appropriate when the capacity to test competence is weak and the consequences of mistakes threaten the individual or others in the community with substantial harm. In such cases, minimum ages may also be necessary to insure that kids grow up a bit before they risk making the *wrong* kind of mistakes. Age-grading isn't so bad after all, if we don't misuse it!

Notes

1. Institute of Judicial Administration/American Bar Association, Juvenile Justice Standards Project, *Rights of Minors, Tentative Draft* (Cambridge, Mass.: Ballinger Publishing

Co., 1977) at 17–32, 119–23; and Alan N. Sussman, *The Rights of Young People* (New York: Avon Books, 1977) at 15–23, 173–92, 220–50.

2. Francis J. Allen, "The Law as a Path to the World," 77 *Michigan Law Review* 157 (1978) at 169.

3. *See* Sussman, *The Rights of Young People, supra* note 1, at 245–46.

4. Sussman, *The Rights of Young People, supra* note 1, at 245–46.

5. *See* Robert Mnookin, *Family and State: Problems and Materials on Children and the Law* (Boston: Little, Brown & Co., 1978) at 668–82.

6. *See Vital Statistics of the United States,* various years from 1946 through 1976, tables on mortality by selected causes of death and age groups.

7. *Vital Statistics of the United States, 1976,* volume II, part A, Table 4–2.

Part IV:
Notes Toward the Future

What the people who are campaigning for an end to sex education in the schools and free contraception information really want is another world. It is a world in which awareness of sex is acquired simultaneously with wisdom teeth, and immediately sanctified by marriage. It is a world that cannot be, and illusions to the contrary, never was. Regret over the sweep of the American sexual revolution is understandable, but reluctance to deal with its consequences is cruel.

Editorial Page, *New York Times*, 1981

The two chapters gathered under the unconfining title of this section are a mix of detail and generality. Chapter 11 applies the approach developed in the previous two sections to the legal and policy dimensions of a specific topic—teenage smoking. This more sustained analysis of one issue as dealt with at various levels of government illustrates the problems and possibilities we encounter when making decisions about youth welfare in real world settings.

Chapter 12 returns to higher levels of generality. I will argue that the messy guesswork we encounter when performing the kind of public policy analysis found in Chapter 11 is the "least worst" method we have to sort out the issues of legal adolescence. The role of law in this setting is modest and reactive. Just as the recent "revolution" in juvenile justice was a reaction to social and political change, future legal policy will probably respond to social reality more than it will function as a catalyst of societal change. Unless, of course, we attempt to use the law to create what the Times *editorial aptly called "another world." Should we succumb to this temptation, the role of law will become at the same time more important and more dangerous.*

Man of Destiny
Smokes because he thinks it's good for his "image." Coughs a lot, too.

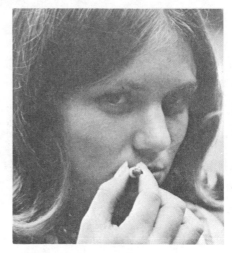

Femme Fatale
Cigarettes are part of the costume. Next week she learns how to inhale.

American Cancer Society, 1967

11

Teenage Smoking: A Public Policy Analysis

Adolescent cigarette smoking is one of the major public health problems of the United States. The vast majority of all adult smokers began their careers with tobacco as teenagers, and most of these adults now regret acquiring this dangerous habit.[1] The sad fact is that discarding a tobacco habit is excruciatingly difficult. If ever an ounce of prevention was the preferred public choice, it is with smoking. Any program that stresses prevention must center its efforts on early and middle adolescence, a period when the public world of the teenager is secondary school.

The range of public policy options and the variety of considerations that should inform public choice in these matters illustrate many of the problems we've been considering. The terms and concepts discussed previously may be of some help in sorting out the proper policy toward adolescent smoking. One begins, hoping for an easy case, by inquiring whether the rebuttable presumption of liberty should here apply. The question is whether there is any good reason not to delegate to 13-, 14-, and 15-year-olds the legal authority to decide whether, when, and how much to smoke.

There are three different, if interrelated, good reasons why we should hesitate before declaring the freedom to smoke a civil liberty for the young. First, the consequences of habitual cigarette smoking are both harmful and difficult to reverse. Second, what the adult world would view as a well-balanced decision on this matter requires a sense of the long-term future not characteristically found in early and middle adolescence. Third, the social context of adolescent decision-making suggests that delegating the decision to smoke to the individual 14-year-old will in fact increase the power of peers and older reference groups to influence individual choice; thus, cigarette smoking may be socially contagious. Each of these assertions deserves amplification.

Evidence implicating smoking as a causal agent in lung cancer and emphysema is overwhelming.[2] The evidence linking smoking to increases in cardiovascular disease is almost as strong.[3] There is also good reason to believe that adult behavior is in great measure dependent on earlier choice: The psychological and physiological consequences of a habit acquired in adolescence make it far more difficult to reverse that behavior later in life.[4] There is, in short, a degree of fatefulness associated with adolescent smoking decisions that is not evident in such matters as voting, choosing styles of dress, or exercising free expression. To discard a smoking habit requires a lot more than changing one's mind.

The fatefulness of the adolescent smoking decision is rendered more troublesome by the absence of abstract and long-term considerations that would normally inform a mature decision. How can one properly convey to a 14-year-old what it means to be dependent on a substance? There is evidence that the social and psychological world of the middle teens is inhospitable to considerations of costs and risks which lie 30 and 40 years in the future.[5] Threatening 14-year-olds with dire warnings about their health at age 50 is not an effective anti-smoking argument. It is also much later in personal development that we come to terms, in any realistic sense, with our own mortality. It is thus unsurprising, but nonetheless sad, that for more than a decade after the *Surgeon General's Report on Smoking and Health,* the propaganda war against cigarettes succeeded in changing adult smoking behavior but has failed miserably with teenagers.[6]

This paradoxical failure to impress the young led, among other things, to redirecting anti-smoking propaganda to the more immediate negative aspects of cigarette smoking portrayed in the advertisement at the beginning of this chapter. Anyone who doubts that kids are different should study the central message with care: the attempt is not to persuade kids that cigarettes are lethal, but rather that they are not "cool." The revised strategy seems to be more successful.

Thus far, we have considered the issue of freedom of choice in smoking as if the costs and benefits inherent in an individual teenager's decision were confined to that individual. There is, however, reason to believe that the expectations and decisions of individual adolescents are dependent upon the behavior, expectations, and values of other adolescents. If this is the case, a worldly public policy must take into account what the effect of conferring freedom of choice on some teenagers will be on the expectations and behavior of other teenagers. To put it bluntly: if your child smokes, the odds increase that mine will too. This introduces a second, more troublesome rationale for limiting the liberty to smoke. To prohibit one child from smoking because a transitional prohibition is in his best interests, is to see that individual child's welfare as the ultimate goal of the system of regulation. To limit liberty as a defense against social contagion is to see the adolescent as part of a group having *collective* "best interests," rather than as an individual with distinct individual interests. In the latter case, the danger of hurting some children in order to benefit others should not be lightly disregarded. Whenever policy decisions are made about adolescent smoking, the universe of teenagers must be divided into adolescents currently smoking and those who do not smoke. It would be fortuitous if the same set of public policies operated to the benefit of both groups, at least in the short term.

The "contagion" rationale is also distinctive because the agents and agencies that socialize adolescents into smoking behavior are not limited to other adolescents. Parents, other adults, and the lords and ladies of Madison Avenue contribute importantly to the expectations and examples which influence smoking decisions among the young. If we are to use public policy towards young people—particularly young smokers—as a means to influence behavior of other young people, there is no neutral principle which would prohibit our attempting to achieve similar ends by regulating the conduct of tobacco companies, advertisers, and adult smokers.

In short, there are important reasons why freedom to smoke cigarettes should not be regarded as a civil liberty that attaches to the early and middle teen years. But that conclusion is only the beginning of the process that should lead to balanced policy. We have already seen, in examining the various rationales for the deregulation of adolescent misdeeds, the social and individual costs of over-zealous prohibitions. The only direct conclusion justified by the analysis so far is that there is no compelling reason for viewing teenage and adult cigarette smoking as identical policy issues. From there, the path to specific public policy is a long one, involving prudential considerations in a real-world setting. What, then, should we do to combat an adolescent smoking epidemic?

Using the criminal law to enforce a general prohibition on cigarette smoking is not a good idea. In principle, the governmental paternalism implicit in an attempt to prohibit adult smoking is an intolerable element of liberal Western democracy, and the influence of adult example on adolescent behavior is too insubstantial to merit an attempt to criminalize such consensual behavior. In practice, a general prohibition of cigarette smoking would produce a wave of deleterious effects that would make us nostalgic for the Volstead Act. Indeed, it seems both ludicrous and irrelevant to discuss such an option in an analysis of legal policy toward young persons. What must be understood, however, is that constraints on formulating policy regarding adolescents are imposed simply by the easy availability of cigarettes for adults. Further, the problems with punishing adult smokers are closely related to the problems associated with punishing active adolescent smokers to protect their non-smoking peers.

If general prohibition is out of the question, what about an age-specific prohibition that attempts to deny access to cigarettes during the early and middle adolescent years, thereby postponing such fateful decisions to more appropriate ages? This is far from a radical suggestion; it is, in formal legal terms, the predominant mode of regulation in the United States today.[7] But it is an extremely porous prohibition. There are billions of cigarettes available to consumers in the United States. Billions. Any prohibitory policy that is based on denying adolescents easy access to cigarettes is doomed to failure. Instead, policy initiatives must seek to reduce adolescent smoking by mild reductions in the availability of cigarettes to teenagers, attempts at dissuasion, punishment of adolescent smokers, limitation of time, place and manner of cigarette use, or some combination of these strategies.

Strategies designed to limit cigarette availability and advertising, to dissuade young persons from smoking, are not particularly troublesome elements of public policy; it is clear, however, that they also are not particularly effective methods of enforcing an age-specific prohibition, at least in the short run.[8] Unless serious penalties are imposed on adults and older adolescents for making cigarettes available to the young, these techniques must be at best a modest part of a comprehensive anti-smoking campaign.

More important policy choices concern the efficacy

and propriety of punishing teenage smokers and the advisability of attempting to prohibit smoking in and around the public schools. It is here that we confront issues that are illuminated, to some degree, by the perspectives discussed earlier. To be specific: What are the principal considerations, pro and con, involved in protecting the young from the deleterious consequences of early cigarette smoking by:

- making cigarette smoking the basis for a juvenile court finding of delinquency, or that the smoker is a "person in need of supervision;"
- sending convicted juvenile smokers to secure or non-secure institutional facilities; or
- suspending or expelling known smokers from public junior and senior high schools?

Well, why not?

It is fashionable to begin the opposition to such social surgery by questioning the efficacy rather than the morality of the process. Surely, such draconian measures can't work. But for present purposes I think it best to assume that this conclusion is both too comforting and too confining. Too comforting because those of the liberal persuasion frequently find themselves reasoning that punitive measures they would object to in any event *won't* work because they *shouldn't* work.[9] Too confining because the conclusion misses an important moral issue. A bloodletting crackdown on smoking in public places and public schools together with vigorous correctional measures might have little impact on already-confirmed smokers. However, it clearly would have some effect on where active smokers pursued their habit, when they smoked, and how their smoking display affected the attitudes and expectations of non-smoking peers. It is, of course, easy to overestimate the deterrent effect of such policies on non-smokers. And the aroma of marijuana is too pervasive these days to dismiss the "forbidden fruit" appeal of prohibited behaviors during adolescence. Still, we know too little of such processes to dismiss out of hand the possible effects of such a serious prohibition policy.[10]

But the efficacy of such policies is beside the point. In former President Nixon's immortal words: "It would be wrong." This judgment is informed, only in part, by the considerations already discussed under the rubric of least harm. To be sure, expulsion from public schools and the use of the machinery of juvenile justice in an anti-smoking crusade would probably produce a classic pattern of costly, intrusive, and near-futile intervention. But it is morally insensitive to reject such measures solely on the basis of cost and benefit. Instead, the case against drastic punishment of adolescent smoking rests on an obligation to preserve the life chances of smoking as well as non-smoking young people. A smoking adolescent is even more at risk than his non-smoking peer who is exposed only to the smoker's exhalations. The harm he does is largely to himself. Drastic intervention of the kind I have suggested merely cuts off his nose to spite his face. To do this in the name of a more general notion of youth welfare is to reinvent the most excessive, punitive, and naive aspects of state interventionist tradition.

A Smokers' Lounge for the High School?

So, where do we go from here? It might be useful to provide an even more specific context in which to consider the residual public choices toward adolescent smoking. To that end, may I put the question of whether the high school in your community should have a smokers' lounge for students? Such an issue may seem mundane, but it is an important example of law and public policy at the tactical level.

Two preliminary observations about the issue deserve mention. First, in the opinion of *this* counsel, the United States Constitution neither compels the establishment of such a lounge (in the name of liberty or youth welfare), nor does it preclude the establishment of the lounge (in the name of parental prerogative). The smokers' lounge debate, like most issues involving regulation of adolescent behavior, is not controlled by the Bill of Rights.

A second interesting feature of the contemporary debate about smokers' lounges is one of context. While the question is frequently debated at the *high school* level, I know of no serious discussion about it in the *junior high schools* of any school district; at the same time, there is no public university that prohibits one. Perhaps this distinction is based upon the differences in smoking behavior between junior high school, high school, and college settings, but I suspect there are deeper reasons why the high school is the usual arena for such debates.

The high school years span the period of early to middle adolescence, when student appeals for autonomy begin to sound authentic. No one of my acquaintance would take a seventh grader's right to smoke at school seriously, but twelfth grade begins to be a different matter. And the four years of public high school encompass ages and grades where we are unprepared to assume that decisions about smoking should be delegated to the students. Most of us would consider it bizarre for a public university to prohibit cigarette smoking; yet opinion among my friends will divide on the high school smokers' lounge. These students are in a middle position. This is one reason why I suspect the smokers' lounge debate at the high school level provides a useful window into the problems of semi-autonomy.

An unromantic assessment of the cost of having or refusing to have a lounge recognizes that the school's capacity to influence adolescent smoking behavior is quite limited. Most of the high school students who would smoke if such a lounge were provided would smoke in any event, either off campus or in the islands of liberty inaccessible to control agencies that are euphemistically termed student rest rooms. Most of the students who would refrain from smoking if no student lounge were available would probably refrain even if the lounge were established. Even if kids survive high school as non-smokers, many will make immature decisions after high school. The impact of public choice is marginal at this level of institutional particularity.

Of equal importance, public institutions must make *some* value judgment on adolescent smoking when the question is as concrete as the smokers' lounge. In making this decision, the high school, or the board of education, or the state legislature cannot remain neutral. To provide such a lounge is to give smoking a form of recognition that is not unimportant. Refusing to provide a smoking lounge or area is attempting to prohibit cigarette smoking in public schools. The prohibition may be relatively toothless, but it constitutes official policy that will produce positive and negative consequences.

What is the case for the smokers' lounge? In any student or faculty debate on the topic I would expect to hear arguments in favor of the lounge that could be clustered under three headings: autonomy, susceptibility to control, and avoidance of the negative consequences of prohibition.

Autonomy Revisited

The autonomy arguments stress the relative maturity of high school students, the unrestricted availability of cigarettes to these students, and the proximity of these students, in age and life situation, to free choices that are available in the adult world. These students will soon be 18 or are already. It is silly and self-defeating to treat them as dependent children. People favoring the lounge will speak of high school seniors. Those opposed will mention high school sophomores.

Many readers may find it incongruous for me to reject a rebuttable presumption of liberty as a general guide to adolescent cigarette smoking and yet to give some credence to arguments for a high school smokers' lounge that are based on notions of student autonomy. But my earlier rejection of a general principle of liberty applies to the whole range of adolescent ages and institutions, while here we deal only with high school students, and the argument that they are close enough to an age of informed free choice has both more specificity and more appeal.

Making Smokers Responsible

Autonomy arguments are a sincerely felt element of the case for decontrol of adolescent smoking behavior, but they cannot decide this issue. More important, I suspect, are the principled and prudent considerations arising from the least harm proposition (Chapter 5). The optimistic side of this argument stresses the gains the high school will experience by first legitimating and then regulating smoking behavior that would occur in any event. Channeling smoking into the lounge will liberate the toilets from near toxic concentrations of smoke. Letting students smoke on campus will keep many student smokers from straying off campus. Indeed, it may keep some students in school. The argument, at its most romantic, holds that giving recognition to students who want to smoke will make them, in their gratitude, more responsible. One can hear the not-so-faint echoes of hope from the debates on the Twenty-sixth Amendment: Extending the franchise to 18-year-olds will clear the streets of violent demonstration. Perhaps.

Doing Less Harm

The more pessimistic (and more persuasive) case for the smokers' lounge rests on the extraordinary costs of attempting to prohibit a widely practiced behavior. First, and of special significance in middle adolescence, to prohibit a behavior is to make violations of that prohibition attractive as forbidden fruit and as an instrument of rebellion.[11] What better way to defy authority than with a cigarette butt? It is unlikely that many high school students take up smoking solely to defy authority, but that may be part of the appeal. Many smoking students will light up on or near high school campuses to express rebellion. It is not unlikely that attempts to prohibit cigarette smoking may increase its incidence and alter the meaning of cigarette smoking behavior among some teenagers.

A related theme is the familiar litany of the costs of "over-criminalization." One of my colleague Norval Morris' favorite phrases is that "you cannot regulate what you prohibit." By driving behavior underground, we destroy the potential of administrative control. By placing cigarette smoking off-limits, we lose an opportunity to see to it that other aspects of student behavior are kept within acceptable boundaries. Once we drive smokers into the toilets or adjacent streets, how can we make sure that marijuana and alcohol are not also consumed?

The Other Side

The case against the smokers' lounge can be summarized by inverting my friend Morris' aphorism: you cannot prohibit what you regulate. Establishing a smokers' lounge gives positive recognition to behavior that is harmful to adolescents, may increase both the number of smokers and the degree of addiction among active smokers, and will likely produce few or none of the benefits promised by its proponents.

The apparent absurdity of allowing early adolescents to obtain contraceptives while prohibiting their sexual activity was justified on the grounds that withholding contraceptives did more harm than good. The opponent of the smokers' lounge suggests that forbidding 15-year-olds access to cigarettes while providing them with a publicly funded, officially approved place to smoke cannot be justified unless it can be demonstrated that a more consistent prohibition policy does more harm than good.

The benefits of prohibition include limiting the social contagion of smoking: My son may still take up cigarettes because he is imitating your son, but this "social learning" will not take place in school. And while the school cannot completely control those who persist in exploring opportunities for smoking on and off its grounds, at least it is not put in the uncomfortable position of advertising a smoking opportunity.

In addition to possibly increasing the number of smokers, establishing a smokers' lounge risks elevating the social status of adolescent smokers and escalating the amount of cigarette smoking among active smokers at a period when this may affect their degree of addiction. The social-standing point is obvious: How can we possibly keep the smokers' lounge from becoming the "in place" for high school students? Keep it small? Kids love to huddle. Make it unpleasant in decor? The adolescent aesthetic is perverse. Rule it off-limits for athletes and cheerleaders? That's discrimination. Restrict access to extremely limited periods? It is very difficult to discern a principle for such a halfway measure.

Next, consider the impact of freely available public school smoking facilities on the number of cigarettes smoked and thus the strength of the habit acquired by active high school smokers. Unless we change our lunch and recess policies, a smokers' lounge provides opportunities to smoke half a pack of cigarettes in the course of a typical school day. Whatever transitory comfort this provides to the student smoker comes at the price of a higher risk of bodily damage during the high school years, and a more extensive habit thereafter.

The anti-lounge lobby would characterize the "benefits" of such a facility as romantic fantasy. Make smokers more responsible, indeed! We are only making smoking respectable. Any serious efforts to regulate smoking behavior in the lounge will drive it back to the washroom and the street. Indeed, whatever moral force the school could bring to bear on enforcing the cigarette prohibition where no lounge is provided is considerably diminished by the "zone defense" of the recognized smoking area. "If I can do it in there, what's so bad about doing it here?" will be the often-heard refrain in the weeks after the lounge opens.

Will the lounge defuse the forbidden fruit appeal of smoking? The grounds and washrooms remain as avenues for rebellion. Moreover, the lounge itself may present the students with an opportunity for expressing rebellion in an area that has become their "turf." One also wonders about the credibility of a public health campaign against cigarette smoking when the school provides facilities for a Marlboro immediately before and after Personal Hygiene 101.

Toothless Prohibition

The question is a close one. As is the case with many public policy questions surrounded by empirical ignorance, the burden of persuasion decides the issue. If our choices were limited to providing a smokers' lounge or expelling cigarette smokers from school, I would opt for the smokers' lounge for students over 16.

But there is a third path: Maintaining the prohibition on smoking and enforcing it with temporary loss of privileges such as participation on athletic teams, and minor inconveniences like detention after school. Under such circumstances I find it hard to conclude with certainty that a prohibition policy does more harm than good.

Perhaps the path I take to these conclusions can best be illustrated by providing three hypothetical cases in which I would come to other conclusions. First, if I were persuaded that a large number of students were leaving high school because of the absence of a smokers' lounge, I would reluctantly change my mind. No matter how foolish the reason, leaving school is too high a price to justify the maintenance of a transitional prohibition. Indeed, it might be prudent to allow those students who have crossed the compulsory school age threshold the opportunity to pursue smoking habits *off campus* during lunch and recess or even in an out-of-doors area on campus in special situations.

Second, if I were in charge of an institution that detained 15- and 16-year-old sentenced juvenile delinquents twenty-four hours a day, I would not attempt to enforce total prohibition on cigarette smoking. This question, too, is close. The great control of a total institution would seem to promise better results for an anti-smoking campaign. However, the risks of further alienating these young persons, who have demonstrated a desperate need for autonomy, makes this a distinguishable case. Smoking isn't the largest problem these kids face. Further, any gains achieved within the institution against an individual's smoking habit would likely disappear the day of his release.

Third, in a situation in which an adolescent is profoundly at risk, I would oppose *any* further sanctions that might increase the peril of that teenager, even if intended as an example to others. The test case is teenage pregnancy. Pregnant girls cannot, in justice, be further punished for the welfare of their more advantaged non-pregnant peers. Even small additional sanctions cannot be justified for those already suffering extreme hardship.

Notes

1. *See* U.S. Public Health Administration Service, *Vital and Health Statistics,* Series 10, Number 59 (1970).
2. *See* U.S. Public Health Service, *Smoking and Health: Report of the Advisory Committee to the Surgeon General of the Public Health Service* (1964); U.S. Public Health Service, *The Facts About Smoking and Health* (1970); and World Health Organization Expert Committee, "Smoking and Its Effects on Health," *World Health Organization Technical Report Series,* No. 551 (1975).
3. Ibid.
4. *See* Richard L. Grant and Morris Weitman, "Cigarette Smoking and School Children: A Longitudinal Study," in *Smoking, Health and Behavior,* Edgar F. Borgatta and Robert R. Evans, eds. (Chicago: Aldine Publishing Co., 1968) at 190 and citations therein.
5. *See* U.S. Department of Health, Education and Welfare, *Teenage Smoking* (1971) at 1–7.
6. *See Teenage Smoking* (1971) at 1–7; Henry Wechsler, *Minimum-Drinking-Age Laws* (Lexington, Mass.: D.C. Heath & Co., 1980) especially chapters 1, 3, and 8.

7. *See* Alan Sussman, *The Rights of Young People* (New York: Avon Books, 1977) Appendix E, at 231–32.

8. *New York Times,* January 15, 1981, at page 20.

9. *See* Franklin E. Zimring and Gordon Hawkins, "Ideology and Euphoria in Crime Control," 10 *Toledo Law Review* 370 (1979) at 378.

10. *See* Franklin E. Zimring and Gordon Hawkins, *Deterrence: The Legal Threat in Crime Control* (Chicago: University of Chicago Press, 1973).

11. *See* Zimring and Hawkins, *Deterrence, supra* note 10, at 92–96 and citations therein.

12

In Praise of Muddling Through

The margin of error in debates such as that over the smokers' lounge is substantial. When an issue is so close and so complicated, why not just flip a coin or hold a referendum? Why not leave it up to the discretion of the high school principal and forget about public policy analysis and social science? The empirical guesses, talmudic distinctions, and analytic pretensions of the smokers' lounge debate provoked one of my most valued colleagues into accusing me of being what he called a little rabbi.[1] He did not mean it as a compliment. He was concerned about the paternalistic assumptions of an academic version of "father knows best," when the truth is that father does not. His position deserves serious attention.

Yet perhaps we learn some things we didn't know

155

before by considering in detail the problem of adolescent cigarette smoking. The debate makes it clear that legal policy toward adolescents is hostage to the kind of life adults lead. One of the reasons that opportunities for regulating adolescent cigarette smoking are so marginal is the prevalence of adult smoking. My guess is that if we ever live in a society where fewer than 20 percent of all parents smoke, the local high school will not have a smokers' lounge, the question will not be a close one, and our capacity to discourage adolescent smoking will be much greater.[2] The problem is that we don't know how to get from where we are to that promised land.

One further example of the hostage problem concerns the availability and social meaning of public transportation as it relates to the minimum age for driving. What are the prospects, in New York City and Los Angeles, for successfully deferring the minimum age, or the average age, for driving until 18?[3] I suspect the prospects of this are much brighter in New York City than in Los Angeles. New York City has good public transportation. In New York, kids can travel *like adults* without driving. In Los Angeles, kids are acutely aware that only kooks, children, and the poor ride the bus. In the San Fernando Valley region of Los Angeles, you cannot really date before you drive. This is not merely a matter of efficient public transportation; it is a function of the social meaning of riding the bus. In New York, adults take the subway. Increase the bus service in Los Angeles, and my guess is that nothing much would happen to the social status of the driver's license. Nothing much will change until adults of all classes and economic groups make taking the bus "respectable."

There is a second dividend that comes from beating an issue to death in the style of our smoking lounge debate. That dividend is insight. By the time we get through with the detailed guesswork and the trade-offs between youth welfare apples and oranges, people may still disagree about whether high schools should have a smokers' lounge, but they will have gained insight about the real reasons we make the choices we do. We will be less likely to take a least harm result, such as smokers' privileges in a detention facility or vaginal foam for the sexually active young, and extrapolate it to general grants of autonomy.

Further, this kind of dialogue should produce the humility that comes with realizing how difficult the difficult cases can be, and how close. We should be better prepared to change our minds when we learn the lessons of experience. If we have to be little rabbis, we should be humble little rabbis. There is one other reason why we must muddle through making guesses about youth welfare: There is no other way. To hold a local election may simply be an efficient way of collecting communal prejudice. And even the best-willed voters may make one of two harmful mistakes: We may make public policy for other people's children in the voting booth; or we may engage in the kind of wishful thinking that led the New York legislature to attempt to legislate virginity by denying contraceptives to kids.

Voting as if we are making laws only for other people's children is always risky. We can see it in the punitive paternalism of the Milwaukee Juvenile Court in the first years of this century. We can see it again in the political rhetoric of the 1980's. This time the problem may be compounded by the fact that our image of other people's children includes a large number of children with dark skins and many who speak Spanish.

The problem is particularly acute in the American city. In New York, more than 60 percent of the people *over* 18 are white and do not have Hispanic surnames. More than 60 percent of the people *under* 18 are non-white or Hispanic.[4] Are these our children, too? Do we really care? Or have declining birthrates, private schools for the middle class, and the capacity to protect our children with private money loosened our ties to the welfare of youth as a public purpose?

The voters also may not wish to confront the real world. It is scary to think of *our* 13- and 14-year-old children taking drugs, drinking, initiating sexual careers, and breaking away too quickly. With the best intentions, we may pass laws that miss the mark because they do not confront reality. Even when we pass laws for our own children, we make avoidable mistakes. And such laws hurt children.

Why not let authority figures make more or less arbitrary decisions in circumstances where we are close to having two right answers; circumstances that approximate those of the smokers' lounge debate? My own conclusion is that this strategy is both unwise and unjust: Unwise because unless we perform serious public policy analysis, we will frequently end up flipping a coin, even where there is one preferable solution but we have not worked hard enough to find it. Unwise also because kids know arbitrary decisions when they see them. Our authority over our adolescent children is tenuous. As a matter of sensible political science, we should attempt to exercise that authority in a visibly credible manner. Candor and consistency may make the high school principal's life harder, but this may be the last best hope for the legitimate authority he needs if the high school is to remain a viable educational institution.

Arbitrary decisions provoke a sense of injustice even if the substantive consequences of such decisions are just as good as the outcomes of a protracted debate. The reason is relatively simple: We owe our children the extra effort of trying to sort things out. This is a debt not easily discharged. I doubt we can ever have a scientific answer to the question of whether the local high school should have a smokers' lounge. But that is no excuse for armchair empiricism and sloppy guessing. We owe our children a rigorous brand of muddling through. Trial and error, mistakes, and injustice in individual cases are inevitable. But the fact that we can never succeed completely is no excuse for not trying.

And that leads me to the semi-final item on my not-so-hidden agenda. This kind of frustrating guesswork is not merely the stuff of the smokers' lounge; it is the stuff of the entire changing legal world of adolescence. This kind of rigorous trial and error is not merely the stuff of the legal world of adolescence; it should be the essence of twentieth century legal method.

Too frequently, the method of academic legal thought has turned to a curious two-stage process: Step One, make up a world. Step Two, make up a set of laws consistent with the world you have made up during Step One. The results are tidy, and the need for research minimal, but this process is either an amusement—a form of jurisprudential chess—or an exercise in self-deception. Grand systems and unitary schemes elude us. We are only human, and we live in a world of other complicated, intractable, various, unpredictable, and unique human beings. To depart the planet we live on when making public policy endangers our children and ouselves.

The litany of impediments that threatens adolescent development is formidable: disorganized families, schools that fail dismally, lack of economic opportunity, and ineffective institutions for work training are some of the tangible problems of the present. Conflict between the generations and the competition between young and old for scarce public resources make matters worse. Social consensus seems an endangered species.

All of these difficulties are mandates for reform and experiment. We cannot solve these problems by legislating adulthood at earlier ages or withdrawing public support for adolescent development. We must come to understand the central importance of a long maturing period for modern liberal democracy. Sustained efforts to improve the transition to adulthood will prove frustrating, expensive—and indispensible—to larger social progress.

Notes

1. Emphatic personal communication from Jerome Kagan, a colleague at the Center for Advanced Studies in the Behavioral Sciences, Stanford, California, in early 1980.
2. *New York Times,* January 15, 1981, at page 20.
3. Leon S. Robertson, "Patterns of Teenaged Driver Involvement in Fatal Motor Vehicle Crashes: Implications for Policy Options," *Journal of Health Politics, Policy & Law,* in press.
4. Trude W. Lash, Heidi Sigal, and Deanna Dudzinski, *State of the Child: New York City II* (New York: Foundation for Child Development, 1980) facing page 128.

Appendix

An Introduction to Legal Reasoning

Throughout this book, in the interest of economy of style, I have paraphrased judicial opinions and statutes. More detailed consideration of specific instances of judicial reasoning would have produced an elephantine volume inaccessible to the wider audience I hope to address.

My professional colleagues can judge whether my interpretation of particular issues is accurate or, at least, fair comment. For those who will use this volume as an introduction to legal studies, however, case materials are a worthwhile supplement to the book. This appendix reproduces relevant sections of *Carey v. Population Services International*. The *Carey* case was selected because of its importance to the least harm argument (Chapter 5). It is also a splendid illustration of the wide diversity of approach and style that results when the Supreme Court (and the nine human beings who sit as judges) struggles with the issues under discussion. Other cases that readers might usefully consult include *In re Gault*, 387 U.S. 1 (1967) and *Goss v. Lopez*, 419 U.S. 565 (1975).

.   .   .

CAREY, GOVERNOR OF NEW YORK, ET AL. *v.* POPU-
LATION SERVICES INTERNATIONAL ET AL.

APPEAL FROM THE UNITED STATES DISTRICT COURT FOR THE
SOUTHERN DISTRICT OF NEW YORK

No. 75–443.   Argued January 10, 1977—Decided June 9, 1977

.   .   .

Opinion of the Court

MR. JUSTICE BRENNAN delivered the opinion of the Court (Parts I, II, III, and V), together with an opinion (Part IV), in which MR. JUSTICE STEWART, MR. JUSTICE MARSHALL, and MR. JUSTICE BLACKMUN joined.

Under New York Educ. Law § 6811 (8) (McKinney 1972) it is a crime (1) for any person to sell or distribute any contraceptive of any kind to a minor under the age of 16 years; (2) for anyone other than a licensed pharmacist to distribute contraceptives to persons 16 or over; and (3) for anyone, including licensed pharmacists, to advertise or display contraceptives.[1] A three-judge District Court for the Southern District of New York declared § 6811 (8) unconstitutional in its entirety under the First and Fourteenth Amendments of the

---

*   *   *   *   *

[1] Section 6811 (8) provides:

"It shall be a class A misdemeanor for:

*   *   *   *   *

"8. Any person to sell or distribute any instrument or article, or any recipe, drug or medicine for the prevention of contraception to a minor under the age of sixteen years; the sale or distribution of such to a person other than a minor under the age of sixteen years is authorized only by a licensed pharmacist but the advertisement or display of said articles, within or without the premises of such pharmacy, is hereby prohibited."

After some dispute in the District Court the parties apparently now agree that Education Law § 6807 (b) (McKinney 1972) constitutes an exception to the distribution prohibitions of § 6811 (8). Section 6807 (b) provides:

"This article shall not be construed to affect or prevent:

*   *   *   *   *

"(b) Any physician . . . who is not the owner of a pharmacy, or registered store, or who is not in the employ of such owner, from supplying his patients with such drugs as the physician . . . deems proper in connection with his practice . . . ."

The definition of "drugs" in Education Law § 6802 (7) (McKinney 1972) apparently includes any contraceptive drug or device. See nn. 7, 13, and 23, and text, *infra*, at 697–699. See also 398 F. Supp. 321, 329–330, and n. 8.

Federal Constitution insofar as it applies to nonprescription contraceptives, and enjoined its enforcement as so applied. 398 F. Supp. 321 (1975). We noted probable jurisdiction, 426 U. S. 918 (1976). We affirm.

I

We must address a preliminary question of the standing of the various appellees to maintain the action. We conclude that appellee Population Planning Associates, Inc. (PPA) has the requisite standing and therefore have no occasion to decide the standing of the other appellees.[2]

PPA is a corporation primarily engaged in the mail-order retail sale of nonmedical contraceptive devices from its offices in North Carolina. PPA regularly advertises its products in periodicals published or circulated in New York, accepts orders from New York residents, and fills orders by mailing contraceptives to New York purchasers. Neither the advertisements nor the order forms accompanying them limit availability of PPA's products to persons of any particular age.

Various New York officials have advised PPA that its activities violate New York law. A letter of December 1, 1971, notified PPA that a PPA advertisement in a New York college newspaper violated § 6811 (8), citing each of the three challenged provisions, and requested "future compliance" with the

---

[2] In addition to PPA, the plaintiffs in the District Court, appellees here, are Population Services International, a nonprofit corporation disseminating birth control information and services; Rev. James B. Hagen, a minister and director of a venereal disease prevention program that distributes contraceptive devices; three physicians specializing in family planning, pediatrics, and obstetrics-gynecology; and an adult New York resident who alleges that the statute inhibits his access to contraceptive devices and information, and his freedom to distribute the same to his minor children. The District Court held that PPA and Hagen had standing, and therefore found it unnecessary to decide the standing of the other plaintiffs. *Id.*, at 327–330.

The appellants here, defendants in the District Court, are state officials responsible for the enforcement of the Education Law provisions.

law.   A second letter, dated February 23, 1973, notifying PPA that PPA's magazine advertisements of contraceptives violated the statute, referred particularly to the provisions prohibiting sales to minors and sales by nonpharmacists, and threatened: "In the event you fail to comply, the matter will be referred to our Attorney General for legal action." Finally, PPA was served with a copy of a report of inspectors of the State Board of Pharmacy, dated September 4, 1974, which recorded that PPA advertised male contraceptives, and had been advised to cease selling contraceptives in violation of the state law.

That PPA has standing to challenge § 6811 (8), not only in its own right but also on behalf of its potential customers, is settled by *Craig* v. *Boren,* 429 U. S. 190, 192–197 (1976). *Craig* held that a vendor of 3.2% beer had standing to challenge in its own right and as advocate for the rights of third persons, the gender-based discrimination in a state statute that prohibited sale of the beer to men, but not to women, between the ages of 18 and 21.   In this case, as did the statute in *Craig,* § 6811 (8) inflicts on the vendor PPA "injury in fact" that satisfies Art. III's case-or-controversy requirement, since "[t]he legal duties created by the statutory sections under challenge are addressed directly to vendors such as [PPA.   It] is obliged either to heed the statutory [prohibition], thereby incurring a direct economic injury through the constriction of [its] market, or to disobey the statutory command and suffer" legal sanctions.   429 U. S., at 194.[3]   There-

---

[3] Appellants contend that PPA has not suffered "injury in fact" because it has not shown that prosecution under § 6811 (8) is imminent. *Steffel* v. *Thompson,* 415 U. S. 452, 459–460 (1974) is dispositive of this argument.   PPA alleges that it has violated the challenged statute in the past, and continues to violate it in the regular course of its business; that it has been advised by the authorities responsible for enforcing the statute that it is in violation; and that on at least one occasion, it has been threatened with prosecution.   The threat is not, as in *Poe* v. *Ullman,* 367 U. S. 497, 508 (1961) (plurality opinion), "chimerical."   In that

fore, PPA is among the "vendors and those in like positions [who] have been uniformly permitted to resist efforts at restricting their operations by acting as advocates for the rights of third parties who seek access to their market or function." *Id.*, at 195.   See also *Eisenstadt* v. *Baird*, 405 U. S. 438, 443–446 (1972) ; *Sullivan* v. *Little Hunting Park*, 396 U. S. 229, 237 (1969) ; *Barrows* v. *Jackson*, 346 U. S. 249, 257–260 (1953). As such, PPA "is entitled to assert those concomitant rights of third parties that would be 'diluted or adversely affected' should [its] constitutional challenge fail."   *Craig* v. *Boren*, *supra*, at 195, quoting *Griswold* v. *Connecticut*, 381 U. S. 479, 481 (1965).[4]

II

Although "[t]he Constitution does not explicitly mention any right of privacy," the Court has recognized that one aspect of the "liberty" protected by the Due Process Clause of the Fourteenth Amendment is "a right of personal privacy, or a guarantee of certain areas or zones of privacy."   *Roe* v. *Wade*, 410 U. S. 113, 152 (1973).   This right of personal privacy includes "the interest in independence in making certain kinds of important decisions."   *Whalen* v. *Roe*, 429 U. S. 589, 599–600 (1977).   While the outer limits of this aspect of privacy have not been marked by the Court, it is clear that among

---

case, the challenged state law had fallen into virtual desuetude through lack of prosecution over some 80 years, and plaintiffs alleged no explicit threat of prosecution. Here, PPA has been threatened with legal action, and prosecutions have been brought under the predecessor of § 6811 (8) as recently as 1965. See, *e. g.*, *People* v. *Baird*, 47 Misc. 2d 478, 262 N. Y. S. 2d 947 (1965).

[4] Indeed, the case for the vendor's standing to assert the rights of potential purchasers of his product is even more compelling here than in *Craig*, because the rights involved fall within the sensitive area of personal privacy. In such a case potential purchasers "may be chilled from . . . assertion [of their own rights] by a desire to protect the very privacy [they seek to vindicate] from the publicity of a court suit." *Singleton* v. *Wulff*, 428 U. S. 106, 117 (1976).

the decisions that an individual may make without unjustified government interference are personal decisions "relating to marriage, *Loving* v. *Virginia*, 388 U. S. 1, 12 (1967); procreation, *Skinner* v. *Oklahoma ex rel. Williamson*, 316 U. S. 535, 541–542 (1942); contraception, *Eisenstadt* v. *Baird*, 405 U. S., at 453–454; *id.*, at 460, 463–465 (WHITE, J., concurring in result); family relationships, *Prince* v. *Massachusetts*, 321 U. S. 158, 166 (1944); and child rearing and education, *Pierce* v. *Society of Sisters*, 268 U. S. 510, 535 (1925); *Meyer* v. *Nebraska*, [262 U. S. 390, 399 (1923)]." *Roe* v. *Wade, supra*, at 152–153. See also *Cleveland Board of Education* v. *LaFleur*, 414 U. S. 632, 639–640 (1974).

The decision whether or not to beget or bear a child is at the very heart of this cluster of constitutionally protected choices. That decision holds a particularly important place in the history of the right of privacy, a right first explicitly recognized in an opinion holding unconstitutional a statute prohibiting the use of contraceptives, *Griswold* v. *Connecticut, supra*, and most prominently vindicated in recent years in the contexts of contraception, *Griswold* v. *Connecticut, supra; Eisenstadt* v. *Baird, supra;* and abortion, *Roe* v. *Wade, supra; Doe* v. *Bolton*, 410 U. S. 179 (1973); *Planned Parenthood of Central Missouri* v. *Danforth*, 428 U. S. 52 (1976). This is understandable, for in a field that by definition concerns the most intimate of human activities and relationships, decisions whether to accomplish or to prevent conception are among the most private and sensitive. "If the right of privacy means anything, it is the right of the individual, married or single, to be free of unwarranted governmental intrusion into matters so fundamentally affecting a person as the decision whether to bear or beget a child." *Eisenstadt* v. *Baird, supra*, at 453. (Emphasis omitted.)

That the constitutionally protected right of privacy extends to an individual's liberty to make choices regarding contraception does not, however, automatically invalidate every state regulation in this area. The business of manufacturing and selling contraceptives may be regulated in ways that do not infringe protected individual choices. And even a burdensome regulation may be validated by a sufficiently compelling state interest. In *Roe* v. *Wade,* for example, after determining that the "right of privacy . . . encompass[es] a woman's decision whether or not to terminate her pregnancy," 410 U. S., at 153, we cautioned that the right is not absolute, and that certain state interests (in that case, "interests in safeguarding health, in maintaining medical standards, and in protecting potential life") may at some point "become sufficiently compelling to sustain regulation of the factors that govern the abortion decision." *Id.,* at 154. "Compelling" is of course the key word; where a decision as fundamental as that whether to bear or beget a child is involved, regulations imposing a burden on it may be justified only by compelling state interests, and must be narrowly drawn to express only those interests. *Id.,* at 155–156, and cases there cited.

With these principles in mind, we turn to the question whether the District Court was correct in holding invalid the provisions of § 6811 (8) as applied to the distribution of nonprescription contraceptives.

III

We consider first the wider restriction on access to contraceptives created by § 6811 (8)'s prohibition of the distribution of nonmedical contraceptives to adults except through licensed pharmacists.

Appellants argue that this Court has not accorded a "right of access to contraceptives" the status of a fundamental aspect of personal liberty. They emphasize that *Griswold* v. *Connecticut* struck down a state prohibition of the *use* of contraceptives, and so had no occasion to discuss laws "regulating their manufacture or sale." 381 U. S., at 485. *Eisenstadt* v. *Baird,* was decided under the Equal Protection Clause, holding that "whatever the rights of the individual to access to contraceptives may be, the rights must be the same for the unmarried and the married alike." 405 U. S., at 453. Thus appellants argue that neither case should be treated as reflecting upon the State's power to limit or prohibit distribution of contraceptives to any persons, married or unmarried. But see *id.*, at 463–464 (WHITE, J., concurring in result).

The fatal fallacy in this argument is that it overlooks the underlying premise of those decisions that the Constitution protects "the right of the individual . . . to be free from unwarranted governmental intrusion into . . . the decision whether to bear or beget a child." *Id.*, at 453. *Griswold* did state that by "forbidding the *use* of contraceptives rather than regulating their manufacture or sale," the Connecticut statute there had "a maximum destructive impact" on privacy rights. 381 U. S., at 485. This intrusion into "the sacred precincts of marital bedrooms" made that statute particularly "repulsive." *Id.*, at 485–486. But subsequent decisions have made clear that the constitutional protection of individual autonomy in matters of childbearing is not dependent on that element. *Eisenstadt* v. *Baird,* holding that the protection is not limited to married couples, characterized the protected right as the "*decision* whether to bear or beget a child." 405 U. S., at 453 (emphasis added). Similarly, *Roe* v. *Wade,* held that the Constitution protects "a woman's *decision* whether or not to terminate her pregnancy." 410 U. S., at 153 (emphasis added). See also *Whalen* v. *Roe, supra,* at 599–600, and n. 26. These decisions put *Griswold* in proper perspective. *Griswold* may no longer be read as holding only that a State may not prohibit a married couple's use of contraceptives. Read in light of its progeny, the teaching of *Griswold* is that the Constitution protects individual decisions in matters of childbearing from unjustified intrusion by the State.

Restrictions on the distribution of contraceptives clearly burden the freedom to make such decisions. A total prohibition against sale of contraceptives, for example, would intrude upon individual decisions in matters of procreation and contraception as harshly as a direct ban on their use. Indeed, in practice, a prohibition against all sales, since more easily and less offensively enforced, might have an even more devastating effect upon the freedom to choose contraception. Cf. *Poe* v. *Ullman*, 367 U. S. 497 (1961).

An instructive analogy is found in decisions after *Roe* v. *Wade, supra,* that held unconstitutional statutes that did not prohibit abortions outright but limited in a variety of ways a woman's access to them. *Doe* v. *Bolton,* 410 U. S. 179 (1973); *Planned Parenthood of Central Missouri* v. *Danforth,* 428 U. S. 52 (1976). See also *Bigelow* v. *Virginia,* 421 U. S. 809 (1975). The significance of these cases is that they establish that the same test must be applied to state regulations that burden an individual's right to decide to prevent conception or terminate pregnancy by substantially limiting access to the means of effectuating that decision as is applied to state statutes that prohibit the decision entirely. Both types of regulation "may be justified only by a 'compelling state interest'. . . and . . . must be narrowly drawn to express only the legitimate state interests at stake." *Roe* v. *Wade, supra,* at 155.[5] See also *Eisenstadt* v. *Baird,* 405 U. S., at 463 (WHITE, J., concurring in result). This is so not because there is an independent fundamental "right of access to contraceptives," but because such access is essential to exercise of the constitutionally protected right of decision in matters of childbearing that is the

---

[5] Contrary to the suggestion advanced in MR. JUSTICE POWELL's opinion, we do not hold that state regulation must meet this standard "whenever it implicates sexual freedom," *post,* at 705, or "affect[s] adult sexual relations," *post,* at 703, but only when it "burden[s] an individual's right to decide to prevent conception or terminate pregnancy by substantially limiting access to the means of effectuating that decision." *Supra,* this page. As we observe below, "the Court has not definitively answered the difficult question whether and to what extent the Constitution prohibits state statutes regulating [private consensual sexual] behavior among adults," n. 17, *infra,* and we do not purport to answer that question now.

underlying foundation of the holdings in *Griswold, Eisenstadt* v. *Baird,* and *Roe* v. *Wade.*

Limiting the distribution of nonprescription contraceptives to licensed pharmacists clearly imposes a significant burden on the right of the individuals to use contraceptives if they choose to do so. *Eisenstadt* v. *Baird, supra,* at 461–464 (WHITE, J., concurring in result). The burden is, of course, not as great as that under a total ban on distribution. Nevertheless, the restriction of distribution channels to a small fraction of the total number of possible retail outlets renders contraceptive devices considerably less accessible to the public, reduces the opportunity for privacy of selection and purchase,[6] and lessens the possibility of price competition.[7] Cf. *Griswold* v. *Connecticut,* 381 U. S., at 503 (WHITE, J., concurring in judgment). Of particular relevance here is *Doe* v. *Bolton, supra,* in which the Court struck down, as unconstitutionally burdening the right of a woman to choose abortion, a statute requiring that abortions be performed only in accredited hospitals, in the absence of proof that the requirement was substantially related to the State's interest in protecting the patient's health. 410 U. S., at 193–195. The same infirmity infuses the limitation in § 6811 (8). "Just as in *Griswold,* where the right of married persons to use contraceptives was 'diluted or adversely affected' by permitting a

---

[6] As MR. JUSTICE POWELL notes, *post,* at 711, the prohibition of mail-order sales of contraceptives, as practiced by PPA, is a particularly "significant invasion of the constitutionally protected privacy in decisions concerning sexual relations."

[7] The narrow exception to § 6811 (8) arguably provided by New York Educ. Law § 6807 (b) (McKinney, Supp. 1976–1977), see n. 1, *supra,* which permits a physician "who is not the owner of a pharmacy, or registered store" to supply his patients with "such drugs as [he] . . . deems proper in connection with his practice" obviously does not significantly expand the number of regularly available, easily accessible retail outlets for nonprescription contraceptives, and so has little relevance to our analysis of this aspect of § 6811 (8).

conviction for giving advice as to its exercise, . . . so here, to sanction a medical restriction upon distribution of a contraceptive not proved hazardous to health would impair the exercise of the constitutional right." *Eisenstadt* v. *Baird*, 405 U. S., at 464 (WHITE, J., concurring in result).

There remains the inquiry whether the provision serves a compelling state interest. Clearly "interests . . . in maintaining medical standards, and in protecting potential life." *Roe* v. *Wade*, 410 U. S., at 154, cannot be invoked to justify this statute. Insofar as § 6811 (8) applies to nonhazardous contraceptives,[8] it bears no relation to the State's interest in protecting health. *Eisenstadt* v. *Baird*, *supra*, at 450–452; 463–464 (WHITE, J., concurring in result).[9] Nor is the interest in protecting potential life implicated in state regulation of contraceptives. *Roe* v. *Wade*, *supra*, at 163–164.

Appellants therefore suggest that § 6811 (8) furthers other state interests. But none of them is comparable to those the Court has heretofore recognized as compelling. Appellants argue that the limitation of retail sales of nonmedical contraceptives to pharmacists (1) expresses "a proper concern that young people not sell contraceptives"; (2) "allows purchasers to inquire as to the relative qualities of the varying products and prevents anyone from tampering with them"; and (3) facilitates enforcement of the other provisions of the statute. Brief for Appellants 14. The first hardly can justify the statute's incursion into constitutionally protected rights, and

---

[8] We have taken judicial notice that "not all contraceptives are potentially dangerous." *Eisenstadt* v. *Baird*, 405 U. S., 438, 451, and n. 9 (1972). See also *id.*, at 463–464 (WHITE, J., concurring in result).

[9] Indeed, in light of other provisions of both federal and state law that comprehensively regulate hazardous drugs and devices, see, *e. g.*, 21 U. S. C. §§ 351–360, especially § 353 (b); N. Y. Educ. Law §§ 6800–6826 (McKinney 1972 and Supp. 1976–1977), especially § 6810, it is unclear what health-related interest the State could have in nonprescription contraceptives. *Eisenstadt* v. *Baird*, *supra*, at 452.

in any event the statute is obviously not substantially related to any goal of preventing young people from selling contraceptives.[10]   Nor is the statute designed to serve as a quality control device.   Nothing in the record suggests that pharmacists are particularly qualified to give advice on the merits of different nonmedical contraceptives, or that such advice is more necessary to the purchaser of contraceptive products than to consumers of other nonprescription items.   Why pharmacists are better able or more inclined than other retailers to prevent tampering with prepackaged products, or, if they are, why contraceptives are singled out for this special protection, is also unexplained.[11]   As to ease of enforcement, the prospect of additional administrative inconvenience has not been thought to justify invasion of fundamental constitutional rights.   See, e. g., *Morrissey* v. *Brewer,* 408 U. S. 471 (1972); *Goldberg* v. *Kelly,* 397 U. S. 254 (1970).

IV [12]

A

The District Court also held unconstitutional, as applied to nonprescription contraceptives, the provision of § 6811 (8) prohibiting the distribution of contraceptives to those under

---

[10] Nothing in New York law limits the employment of minors who work as sales clerks in pharmacies.   To the extent that minors employed in other retail stores selling contraceptive products might be exposed "to undesirable comments and gestures," Brief for Appellants 3–4, or otherwise corrupted by exposure to such products, minors working as sales clerks in pharmacies are exposed to the same hazards.

[11] As the District Court pointed out, while these interests are insufficient to justify limiting the distribution of nonhazardous contraceptives to pharmacists, other restrictions may well be reasonably related to the objective of quality control.   We therefore express no opinion on, for example, restrictions on the distribution of contraceptives through vending machines, which are not before us in this case. See 398 F. Supp., at 336.

[12] This part of the opinion expresses the views of JUSTICES BRENNAN, STEWART, MARSHALL, and BLACKMUN.

16 years of age.[13]   Appellants contend that this provision of the statute is constitutionally permissible as a regulation of the morality of minors, in furtherance of the State's policy against promiscuous sexual intercourse among the young.

The question of the extent of state power to regulate conduct of minors not constitutionally regulable when committed by adults is a vexing one, perhaps not susceptible of precise answer. We have been reluctant to attempt to define "the totality of the relationship of the juvenile and the state." *In re Gault,* 387 U. S. 1, 13 (1967). Certain principles, however, have been recognized. "Minors, as well as adults, are protected by the Constitution and possess constitutional rights." *Planned Parenthood of Central Missouri* v. *Danforth,* 428 U. S., at 74. "[W]hatever may be their precise impact, neither the Fourteenth Amendment nor the Bill of Rights is for adults alone." *In re Gault, supra,* at 13.[14]   On the other hand, we have held in a variety of contexts that "the power of the state to control the conduct of children reaches beyond the scope of its authority over adults." *Prince* v. *Massachusetts,* 321 U. S. 158, 170 (1944). See *Ginsberg* v. *New York,* 390 U. S. 629 (1968). See also *McKeiver* v. *Pennsylvania,* 403 U. S. 528 (1971).

---

[13] Subject to an apparent exception for distribution by physicians in the course of their practice. See n. 1, *supra,* and *infra,* at 697–699, and n. 23.

[14] Thus minors are entitled to constitutional protection for freedom of speech, *Tinker* v. *Des Moines School Dist.,* 393 U. S. 503 (1969); *West Virginia Bd. of Education* v. *Barnette,* 319 U. S. 624 (1943); equal protection against racial discrimination, *Brown* v. *Board of Education,* 347 U. S. 483 (1954); due process in civil contexts, *Goss* v. *Lopez,* 419 U. S. 565 (1975); and a variety of rights of defendants in criminal proceedings, including the requirement of proof beyond a reasonable doubt, *In re Winship,* 397 U. S. 358 (1970), the prohibition of double jeopardy, *Breed* v. *Jones,* 421 U. S. 519 (1975), the rights to notice, counsel, confrontation, and cross-examination, and not to incriminate oneself, *In re Gault,* 387 U. S. 1 (1967), and the protection against coerced confessions, *Gallegos* v. *Colorado,* 370 U. S. 49 (1962); *Haley* v. *Ohio,* 332 U. S. 596 (1948).

Of particular significance to the decision of this case, the right to privacy in connection with decisions affecting procreation extends to minors as well as to adults. *Planned Parenthood of Central Missouri* v. *Danforth, supra,* held that a State "may not impose a blanket provision . . . requiring the consent of a parent or person *in loco parentis* as a condition for abortion of an unmarried minor during the first 12 weeks of her pregnancy." 428 U. S., at 74. As in the case of the spousal-consent requirement struck down in the same case, *id.,* at 67–72, "the State does not have the constitutional authority to give a third party an absolute, and possibly arbitrary, veto," *id.,* at 74, " 'which the state itself is absolutely and totally prohibited from exercising.' " *Id.,* at 69. State restrictions inhibiting privacy rights of minors are valid only if they serve "any significant state interest . . . that is not present in the case of an adult." *Id.,* at 75.[15] *Planned Parenthood* found that no such interest justified a state requirement of parental consent.[16]

---

[15] This test is apparently less rigorous than the "compelling state interest" test applied to restrictions on the privacy rights of adults. See, *e. g.,* n. 16, *infra.* Such lesser scrutiny is appropriate both because of the States' greater latitude to regulate the conduct of children, *Prince* v. *Massachusetts,* 321 U. S. 158 (1944); *Ginsberg* v. *New York,* 390 U. S. 629 (1968), and because the right of privacy implicated here is "the interest in independence in making certain kinds of important decisions," *Whalen* v. *Roe,* 429 U. S. 589, 599–600 (1977), and the law has generally regarded minors as having a lesser capability for making important decisions. See, *e. g., Planned Parenthood,* 428 U. S., at 102 (STEVENS, J., concurring in part and dissenting in part).

[16] *Planned Parenthood,* however, "does not suggest that every minor, regardless of age or maturity, may give effective consent for termination of her pregnancy. See *Bellotti* v. *Baird,* [428 U. S. 132 (1976)]. The fault of [the particular statute considered in *Planned Parenthood*] is that it imposes a special-consent provision, exercisable by a person other than the woman and her physician, as a prerequisite to a minor's termination of her pregnancy . . . without a sufficient justification for the restriction." *Id.,* at 75.

Since the State may not impose a blanket prohibition, or even a blanket requirement of parental consent, on the choice of a minor to terminate her pregnancy, the constitutionality of a blanket prohibition of the distribution of contraceptives to minors is *a fortiori* foreclosed. The State's interests in protection of the mental and physical health of the pregnant minor, and in protection of potential life are clearly more implicated by the abortion decision than by the decision to use a nonhazardous contraceptive.

Appellants argue, however, that significant state interests are served by restricting minors' access to contraceptives, because free availability to minors of contraceptives would lead to increased sexual activity among the young, in violation of the policy of New York to discourage such behavior.[17] The argument is that minors' sexual activity may be deterred by increasing the hazards attendant on it. The same argument, however, would support a ban on abortions for minors, or indeed support a prohibition on abortions, or access to contraceptives, for the unmarried, whose sexual activity is also against the public policy of many States. Yet, in each of these areas, the Court has rejected the argument, noting in *Roe* v. *Wade*, that "no court or commentator has taken the argument seriously."   410

---

[17] Appellees argue that the State's policy to discourage sexual activity of minors is itself unconstitutional, for the reason that the right to privacy comprehends a right of minors as well as adults to engage in private consensual sexual behavior. We observe that the Court has not definitively answered the difficult question whether and to what extent the Constitution prohibits state statutes regulating such behavior among adults. See generally Note, On Privacy: Constitutional Protection for Personal Liberty, 48 N. Y. U. L. Rev. 670, 719–738 (1973). But whatever the answer to that question, *Ginsberg* v. *New York, supra*, indicates that in the area of sexual mores, as in other areas, the scope of permissible state regulation is broader as to minors than as to adults. In any event, it is unnecessary to pass upon this contention of appellees, and our decision proceeds on the assumption that the Constitution does not bar state regulation of the sexual behavior of minors.

U. S., at 148. The reason for this unanimous rejection was stated in *Eisenstadt* v. *Baird:* "It would be plainly unreasonable to assume that [the State] has prescribed pregnancy and the birth of an unwanted child [or the physical and psychological dangers of an abortion] as punishment for fornication." 405 U. S., at 448. We remain reluctant to attribute any such "scheme of values" to the State.[18]

Moreover, there is substantial reason for doubt whether limiting access to contraceptives will in fact substantially discourage early sexual behavior. Appellants themselves conceded in the District Court that "there is no evidence that teenage extramarital sexual activity increases in proportion to the availability of contraceptives," 398 F. Supp., at 332, and n. 10, and accordingly offered none, in the District Court or here. Appellees, on the other hand, cite a considerable body of evidence and opinion indicating that there is no such deterrent effect.[19] Although we take judicial notice, as did the

---

[18] We note, moreover, that other provisions of New York law argue strongly against any conclusion that the deterrence of illegal sexual conduct among minors was an objective of § 6811 (8). First, a girl in New York may marry as young as 14, with the consent of her parents and a family court judge. N. Y. Dom. Rel. Law §§ 15–a, 15 (2), 15 (3) (McKinney 1964 and Supp. 1976–1977). Yet although sexual intercourse by a married woman of that age violates no state law, § 6811 (8) prohibits distribution of contraceptives to her. Second, New York requires that birth control information and services be provided to recipients of certain welfare programs, provided only that they are "of childbearing age, including children who can be considered sexually active." N. Y. Soc. Serv. Law § 350 (1)(e) (McKinney 1976); cf. 42 U. S. C. § 602 (a)(15)(A) (1970 ed., Supp. V). See also N. Y. Soc. Serv. Law § 365–a (3)(c) (McKinney 1976); cf. 42 U. S. C. § 1396d (a)(vii)(4)(C) (1970 ed., Supp. V). Although extramarital intercourse is presumably as contrary to state policy among minors covered by those programs as among others, state law requires distribution of contraceptives to them and prohibits their distribution to all others.

[19] See, *e. g.,* Settlage, Baroff, & Cooper, Sexual Experience of Younger Teenage Girls Seeking Contraceptive Assistance for the First Time, Family Planning Perspectives 223 (fall 1973); Pilpel & Wechsler, Birth Control,

District Court, *id.*, at 331–333, that with or without access to contraceptives, the incidence of sexual activity among minors is high,[20] and the consequences of such activity are frequently devastating,[21] the studies cited by appellees play no part in our decision. It is enough that we again confirm the principle that when a State, as here, burdens the exercise of a fundamental right, its attempt to justify that burden as a rational means for the accomplishment of some significant state policy requires more than a bare assertion, based on a conceded complete absence of supporting evidence, that the burden is connected to such a policy.[22]

Teenagers and the Law: A New Look 1971, Family Plannning Perspectives 37 (July 1971); Stein, Furnishing Information and Medical Treatment to Minors for Prevention, Termination and Treatment of Pregnancy, Clearinghouse Review 131, 132 (July 1971); Reiss, Contraceptive Information and Sexual Morality, Journal of Sex Research 51 (Apr. 1966). See also Note, Parental Consent Requirements and Privacy Rights of Minors: The Contraceptive Controversy, 88 Harv. L. Rev. 1001, 1010, and n. 67 (1975); Jordan, A Minor's Right to Contraceptives, 7 U. Calif. Davis L. Rev. 270, 272–273 (1974).

[20] See, *e. g., id.*, at 271–273; Kanter & Zelnick, Sexual Experience of Young Unmarried Women in the United States, Family Planning Perspectives 9 (Oct. 1972).

[21] Although this is not the occasion for a full examination of these problems, the following data sketchily indicate their extent. According to New York City Department of Health statistics, filed with the Court by the American Civil Liberties Union as *amicus curiae*, in New York City alone there were over 6,000 live births to girls under the age of 17 in 1975, as well as nearly 11,000 abortions. Moreover, "[t]eenage motherhood involves a host of problems, including adverse physical and psychological effects upon the minor and her baby, the continuous stigma associated with unwed motherhood, the need to drop out of school with the accompanying impairment of educational opportunities, and other dislocations [including] forced marriage of immature couples and the often acute anxieties involved in deciding whether to secure an abortion." Note, Parental Consent Requirements and Privacy Rights of Minors: The Contraceptive Controversy, 88 Harv. L. Rev. 1001, 1010 (1975) (footnotes omitted). See also Jordan, *supra*, n. 19, at 273–275.

[22] Appellants argue that the statement in *Ginsberg* v. *New York*, 390

B

Appellants argue that New York does not totally prohibit distribution of contraceptives to minors under 16, and that accordingly § 6811 (8) cannot be held unconstitutional. Although § 6811 (8) on its face is a flat unqualified prohibition, Educ. Law § 6807 (b) (McKinney, Supp. 1976–1977), see nn. 1, 7, and 13, *supra*, provides that nothing in Education Law §§ 6800–6826 shall be construed to prevent "[a]ny physician . . . from supplying his patients with such drugs as [he] . . . deems proper in connection with his practice." This narrow exception, however, does not save the statute. As we have held above as to limitations upon distribution to adults, less than total restrictions on access to contraceptives that significantly burden the right to decide whether to bear children must also pass constitutional scrutiny. Appellants assert no medical necessity for imposing a medical limitation on the distribution of nonprescription contraceptives to minors. Rather, they argue that such a restriction serves to emphasize to young people the seriousness with which the State views the decision to engage in sexual intercourse at an early age.[23] But this is only another form of the

---

U. S., at 641, that "it was not irrational for the legislature to find that exposure to material condemned by the statute is harmful to minors," is authority that the burden is appellees' to prove that there is no connection between the statute and the asserted state policy. But *Ginsberg* concerned a statute prohibiting dissemination of obscene material that it held was not constitutionally protected. In contrast § 6811 (8) concerns distribution of material access to which is essential to exercise of a fundamental right.

[23] There is considerable doubt that appellants accurately identify the legislative purposes in enacting Educ. Law §§ 6807 (b) and 6811 (8). Section 6811 (8) (formerly Educ. Law § 6804–b and before that Penal Law § 1142 (2)) was first enacted in 1965 as a modification, apparently in response to *Griswold* v. *Connecticut*, 381 U. S. 479 (1965), of former Penal Law § 1142, titled "Indecent articles." 1965 N. Y. Laws, c. 637. This statute, which dated back at least to § 318 of the Penal Code of

argument that juvenile sexual conduct will be deterred by
making contraceptives more difficult to obtain. Moreover,
that argument is particularly poorly suited to the restriction

---

1881, 1881 N. Y. Laws, c. 676, had made it a misdemeanor for any
person to distribute or advertise "any instrument or article, or any drug
or medicine, for the prevention of conception." Section 6807 (b), on the
other hand, generally excepts the distribution of drugs by a physician in
the course of his practice from all the licensing requirements and
restrictions imposed on the practice of pharmacy by Education Law
§§ 6800–6826 (subject to certain provisos not here relevant). Such a
provision, in one form or another and bearing several different numbers,
has been included in the article concerning the practice of pharmacy since
that article was first incorporated in the Education Law in 1927, see
former Education Law § 1361, 1927 N. Y. Laws, c. 85, and before
that a similar provision was included in the statutes regulating pharmacy
in the Public Health Law. See, e. g., Public Health Law of 1893, § 187,
1893 N. Y. Laws, c. 661. Thus, § 6807 (b) and its predecessors long
predate the inclusion of § 6811 (8) in the Education Law.

Even more significantly, when § 6811 (8) was first enacted as Penal
Law § 1142 (2), it was not subject to the physicians' exception of § 6807
(b). Rather, it was apparently subject to a different physicians' exception, former Penal Law § 1145 (§ 321 of the Penal Code of 1881), which
provided:

"An article or instrument, used or applied by physicians lawfully practicing, or by their direction or prescription, for the cure or prevention of
disease, is not an article of indecent or immoral nature or use, within this
chapter. The supplying of such articles to such physicians or by their
direction or prescription, is not an offense under this chapter."

This was interpreted by the New York Court of Appeals to permit a
physician "in good faith" to use contraceptives to treat "a married person
to cure or prevent disease," but not to permit "promiscuous advice to
patients irrespective of their condition." People v. Sanger, 222 N. Y. 192,
194–195, 118 N. E. 637, 637–638 (1918), appeal dismissed for lack of
jurisdiction, 251 U. S. 537 (1919) (per curiam). See also People v. Byrne,
99 Misc. 1, 163 N. Y. S. 682 (1917); People v. Baird, 47 Misc. 2d 478, 262
N. Y. S. 2d 947 (1965).

In light of this history, it appears that insofar as the legislature had
§ 6807 (b) in mind at all when it transferred the prohibition of distribu-

appellants are attempting to justify, which on appellants' construction delegates the State's authority to disapprove of minors' sexual behavior to physicians, who may exercise it arbitrarily,[24] either to deny contraceptives to young people, or to undermine the State's policy of discouraging illicit early sexual behavior. This the State may not do. Cf. *Planned Parenthood of Central Missouri v. Danforth*, 428 U. S., at 69, 74.[25]

---

tion of contraceptives to those under 16 from the Penal Law to the Education Law, it thought of that section as at most a narrow exception, analogous to § 1145, permitting physicians, "in connection with [their] practice," to treat or prevent disease, rather than, as appellants assert, intending that §§ 6807 (b) and 6811 (8) be read together as establishing a scheme under which contraceptives would be freely available to those under 16, but limiting the distribution function to physicians. The legislative history of attempts in 1972 and 1974 to modify § 6811 (8), to which appellants refer, supports this construction. The legislators debating those bills seem to have thought of § 6811 (8) as a flat prohibition of the distribution of contraceptives to minors, and made no reference to § 6807 (b).

[24] In *Doe v. Bolton*, 410 U. S. 179, 196 (1973), we doubted that physicians would allow their moral "predilections on extramarital sex" to interfere with their medical judgments concerning abortions. Here, however, no *medical* judgment is involved at all; the State purports to commission physicians to engage in *moral* counseling that can reflect little other than their private views on the morality of premarital sex among the young. It seems evident that many physicians are likely to have views on this subject to a significant degree more permissive or more restrictive than those of the State, the minor, or the minor's parents. Moreover, nothing in § 6807 (b) suggests that the role of the physician is limited to such "counseling." The statute does nothing more than to permit the physician to provide his patients with such drugs or devices as he "deems proper." Such "absolute, and possibly arbitrary" discretion over the privacy rights of minors is precisely what *Planned Parenthood* condemned. 428 U. S., at 74.

[25] In cases involving abortions, we have emphasized that the decision to terminate a pregnancy is properly made by a woman in consultation with her physician. See, *e. g.*, *Roe v. Wade*, 410 U. S. 113, 153, 164 (1973); *Planned Parenthood of Central Missouri v. Danforth*, 428 U. S.,

V

The District Court's holding that the prohibition of any "advertisement or display" of contraceptives is unconstitutional was clearly correct. Only last Term *Virginia Pharmacy Bd.* v. *Virginia Citizens Consumer Council,* 425 U. S. 748 (1976), held that a State may not "completely suppress the dissemination of concededly truthful information about entirely lawful activity," even when that information could be categorized as "commercial speech." *Id.,* at 773. Just as in that case, the statute challenged here seeks to suppress completely any information about the availability and price of contraceptives.[26] Nor does the case present any question left open in *Virginia Pharmacy Bd.;* here, as there, there can be no contention that the regulation is "a mere time, place, and manner restriction," *id.,* at 771, or that it prohibits only misleading or deceptive advertisements, *ibid.,* or "that the transactions proposed in the forbidden advertisements are themselves illegal in any way. Cf. *Pittsburgh Press Co.* v. *Human Relations Comm'n,* [413 U. S. 376 (1973)]." *Id.,* at 772–773. Moreover, in addition to the "substantial individual and societal interests" in the free flow of commercial information enumerated in *Virginia Pharmacy Bd., supra,* at 763–766, the

---

at 75. No such suggestion, however, has been made concerning the right to obtain or use contraceptives. See *Griswold* v. *Connecticut, supra; Eisenstadt* v. *Baird,* 405 U. S. 438 (1972). The reason, of course, is that the abortion decision necessarily involves a medical judgment, *Roe* v. *Wade, supra,* at 164, while the decision to use a nonhazardous contraceptive does not. *Eisenstadt* v. *Baird, supra,* at 463–464 (WHITE, J., concurring in result). See also n. 24, *supra.*

[26] The prohibition of advertising and display of contraceptives is invalid as to prescription as well as nonprescription contraceptives, at least when the advertising is by persons who are licensed to sell such products. *Virginia Pharmacy Bd.* v. *Virginia Citizens Consumer Council,* 425 U. S. 748 (1976).

information suppressed by this statute "related to activity with which, at least in some respects, the State could not interfere." 425 U. S., at 760. Cf. *Bigelow* v. *Virginia,* 421 U. S. 809 (1975).

Appellants contend that advertisements of contraceptive products would be offensive and embarrassing to those exposed to them, and that permitting them would legitimize sexual activity of young people. But these are classically not justifications validating the suppression of expression protected by the First Amendment. At least where obscenity is not involved, we have consistently held that the fact that protected speech may be offensive to some does not justify its suppression. See, *e. g., Cohen* v. *California,* 403 U. S. 15 (1971).[27] As for the possible "legitimation" of illicit sexual behavior, whatever might be the case if the advertisements directly incited illicit sexual activity among the young, none of the advertisements in this record can even remotely be characterized as "directed to inciting or producing imminent lawless action and . . . likely to incite or produce such action." *Brandenburg* v. *Ohio,* 395 U. S. 444, 447 (1969). They merely state the availability of products and services that are not only entirely legal, cf. *Pittsburgh Press Co.* v. *Human Relations Comm'n,* 413 U. S. 376 (1973), but constitutionally protected. Cf. *Bigelow* v. *Virginia, supra.*[28] These arguments

---

[27] Indeed, as the Court recognized in *Virginia Pharmacy Bd.,* much advertising is "tasteless and excessive," and no doubt offends many. 425 U. S., at 765.

[28] Appellants suggest no distinction between commercial and noncommercial speech that would render these discredited arguments meritorious when offered to justify prohibitions on commercial speech. On the contrary, such arguments are clearly directed not at any commercial aspect of the prohibited advertising but at the ideas conveyed and form of expression—the core of First Amendment values. Cf. *Linmark Associates, Inc.* v. *Willingboro, ante,* at 96–97.

therefore do not justify the total suppression of advertising concerning contraceptives.[29]

Affirmed.

THE CHIEF JUSTICE dissents.

MR. JUSTICE WHITE, concurring in part and concurring in the result.

I join Parts I, III, and V of the Court's opinion and concur in the result with respect to Part IV.*

Although I saw no reason in *Eisenstadt* v. *Baird,* 405 U. S. 438 (1972), to reach "the novel constitutional question whether a State may restrict or forbid the distribution of contraceptives to the unmarried," *id.,* at 465 (concurring in result), four of the seven Justices participating in that case held that in this respect the rights of unmarried persons were equal to those of the married. Given *Eisenstadt* and given the decision of the Court in the abortion case, *Roe* v. *Wade,* 410 U. S. 113 (1973), the result reached by the Court in Part III of its opinion appears warranted. I do not regard the opinion, however, as declaring unconstitutional any state law forbidding extramarital sexual relations. On this assumption I join Part III.

I concur in the result in Part IV primarily because the State has not demonstrated that the prohibition against distribution of contraceptives to minors measurably contributes to the deterrent purposes which the State advances as justification for the restriction. Again, however, the legality of state laws forbidding premarital intercourse is not at issue here; and, with MR. JUSTICE STEVENS, "I would describe as

---

[29] We do not have before us, and therefore express no views on, state regulation of the time, place, or manner of such commercial advertising based on these or other state interests.

*There is no need for present purposes to agree or disagree with the Court's summary of the law expressed in Part II.

'frivolous' appellees' argument that a minor has the constitutional right to put contraceptives to their intended use, notwithstanding the combined objection of both parents and the State," *post,* at 713.

In joining Part V of the Court's opinion, I should also say that I agree with the views of MR. JUSTICE STEVENS expressed in Part II of his separate opinion.

MR. JUSTICE POWELL, concurring in part and concurring in the judgment.

I agree that Population Planning Associates has standing to maintain this action, and therefore join Part I of the Court's opinion.   Although I concur in the judgment of the Court, I am not persuaded that the Constitution requires the severe constraints that the Court's opinion places upon legislative efforts to regulate the distribution of contraceptives, particularly to the young.

I

The Court apparently would subject all state regulation affecting adult sexual relations to the strictest standard of judicial review.   Under today's decision, such regulation "may be justified only by compelling state interests, and must be narrowly drawn to express only those interests."   *Ante,* at 686. Even regulation restricting only the sexual activity of the young must now be justified by a "significant state interest," a standard that is "apparently less rigorous" than the standard the Court would otherwise apply.   *Ante,* at 693 n. 15.   In my view, the extraordinary protection the Court would give to all personal decisions in matters of sex is neither required by the Constitution nor supported by our prior decisions.

A

The cases on which the Court relies for its "compelling interest" standard do not support the sweeping principle it adopts today.   Those cases generally involved direct and substantial interference with constitutionally protected rights. In *Griswold* v. *Connecticut*, 381 U. S. 479 (1965), the Court invalidated a state statute prohibiting the use of contraceptives and making it illegal for physicians to give advice to married persons regarding contraception. The statute was viewed as one "operat[ing] directly on an intimate relation of husband and wife and their physician's role in one aspect of that relation," *id.*, at 482, and "seek[ing] to achieve its goals by means having a maximum destructive impact upon that relationship," *id.*, at 485. In *Roe* v. *Wade*, 410 U. S. 113 (1973) the Court reviewed a Texas statute imposing severe criminal sanctions on physicians and other medical personnel who performed nontherapeutic abortions, thus effectively foreclosing the availability and safety of this desired service. And just last Term, in *Planned Parenthood of Central Missouri* v. *Danforth*, 428 U. S. 52 (1976), we invalidated Missouri's requirement of spousal consent as a state-imposed "absolute obstacle to a woman's decision that *Roe* held to be constitutionally protected from such interference." *Id.*, at 71 n. 11.

The Court relies on *Planned Parenthood, supra*, and *Doe* v. *Bolton*, 410 U. S. 179 (1973), for the proposition that "the same test must be applied to state regulations that burden an individual's right to decide to prevent conception or terminate pregnancy by substantially limiting access to the means of effectuating that decision as is applied to state statutes that prohibit the decision entirely." *Ante*, at 688. But neither of those cases refers to the "compelling state interest" test. In *Bolton*, the Court invalidated procedural requirements of the Georgia abortion statute that were found not "reasonably related" to the asserted legislative purposes or to the "patient's needs." 410 U. S., at 194, 199. *Planned Parenthood* involved—in addition to the "absolute obstacle" referred to above—the Missouri requirement of prior written consent by the pregnant woman. Despite the fact that Missouri normally did not require written consent for other surgical procedures, the Court sustained this regulation without requiring any demonstration of compelling state interests. The Court recognized that the decision to abort "is an important, and often a stressful one," and the State thus constitutionally could assure that the woman was aware of the significance of the decision. 428 U. S., at 67.

In sum, the Court quite unnecessarily extends the reach of cases like *Griswold* and *Roe*. Neither our precedents nor sound principles of constitutional analysis require state legislation to meet the exacting "compelling state interest" standard whenever it implicates sexual freedom. In my view, those cases make clear that that standard has been invoked only when the state regulation entirely frustrates or heavily burdens the exercise of constitutional rights in this area. See *Bellotti* v. *Baird*, 428 U. S. 132, 147 (1976). This is not to say that other state regulation is free from judicial review. But a test so severe that legislation rarely can meet it should be imposed by courts with deliberate restraint in view of the respect that properly should be accorded legislative judgments.

B

There is also no justification for subjecting restrictions on the sexual activity of the young to heightened judicial review. Under our prior cases, the States have broad latitude to legislate with respect to adolescents. The principle is well settled that "a State may permissibly determine that, at least in some precisely delineated areas, a child . . . is not possessed of that full capacity for individual choice" which is essential to the exercise of various constitutionally protected interests. *Ginsberg* v. *New York*, 390 U. S. 629, 649–650 (1968) (STEWART, J., concurring in result). This principle is the premise of our prior decisions, ostensibly reaffirmed by the plurality, *ante*, at 692, holding that "the power of the state to control the conduct of children reaches beyond the scope of its authority over adults." *Prince* v. *Massachusetts*, 321 U. S. 158, 170 (1944).

Restraints on the freedom of minors may be justified "even though comparable restraints on adults would be constitutionally impermissible." *Planned Parenthood of Central Missouri* v. *Danforth, supra,* at 102 (STEVENS, J., concurring in part and dissenting in part).[1]

New York has exercised its responsibility over minors in areas falling within the "cluster of constitutionally protected choices" relating to sex and marriage. *Ante,* at 685. It has set an age limitation below which persons cannot marry without parental consent, N. Y. Dom. Rel. Law §§ 15, 15–a (McKinney 1964 and Supp. 1976–1977), and has established by statute the age at which a minor is legally recognized as having the capacity to consent to sexual activity, Penal Law § 130.05 (3) (a) (McKinney 1975). See also Penal Law §§ 130.25, 130.30, 130.35 (McKinney 1975). These provisions highlight the State's concern that its juvenile citizens generally lack the maturity and understanding necessary to make decisions concerning marriage and sexual relationships.

Until today, I would not have thought it was even arguably necessary to review state regulation of this sort under a standard that for all practical purposes approaches the "compelling state interest" standard. At issue in *Ginsberg* v. *New York, supra,* for example, was the question of the constitutionality on its face of a New York criminal obscenity statute which prohibited the sale to minors of material defined to be obscene on the basis of its appeal to them whether or not it would be obscene to adults. The Court recognized that "the State has

---

[1] MR. JUSTICE STEVENS recently provided the following examples, deeply rooted in our traditions and law:

"Because he may not foresee the consequences of his decision, a minor may not make an enforceable bargain. He may not lawfully work or travel where he pleases, or even attend exhibitions of constitutionally protected adult motion pictures. Persons below a certain age may not marry without parental consent. Indeed, such consent is essential even when the young woman is already pregnant." 428 U. S., at 102.

an interest 'to protect the welfare of children' and to see that
they are 'safeguarded from abuses' which might prevent their
'growth into free and independent well-developed men and
citizens.' "   390 U. S., at 640–641, quoting *Prince* v. *Massachusetts, supra,* at 165.   Consequently, the "only question
remaining" in that case was "whether the New York Legislature might rationally conclude. as it has, that exposure to the
materials proscribed by [the statute] constitutes such an
'abuse.' "   390 U. S., at 641.   Similarly, the relevant question
in any case where state laws impinge on the freedom of action
of young people in sexual matters is whether the restriction
rationally serves valid state interests.

II

With these considerations in mind, I turn to the specific
provisions of the New York statute limiting the distribution
of contraceptives.

A

New York has made it a crime for anyone other than a
physician to sell or distribute contraceptives to minors under
the age of 16 years.   Educ. Law § 6811 (8) (McKinney 1972).
This element of New York's program of regulation for the
protection of its minor citizens is said to evidence the State's
judgment that the health and well-being of minors would be
better assured if they are not encouraged to engage in sexual
intercourse without guidance.   Although I have no doubt that
properly framed legislation serving this purpose would meet
constitutional standards, the New York provision is defective
in two respects.   First, it infringes the privacy interests
of married females between the ages of 14 and 16, see
ante, at 695 n. 18, in that it prohibits the distribution of
contraceptives to such females except by a physician.   In
authorizing marriage at that age, the State also sanctions
sexual intercourse between the partners and expressly recognizes that once the marriage relationship exists the husband and

wife are presumed to possess the requisite understanding and maturity to make decisions concerning sex and procreation. Consequently, the state interest that justifies a requirement of prior counseling with respect to minors in general simply is inapplicable with respect to minors for whom the State has affirmatively approved marriage.

Second, this provision prohibits parents from distributing contraceptives to their children, a restriction that unjustifiably interferes with parental interests in rearing their children. Cf. *Ginsberg* v. *New York,* 390 U. S., at 639 and n. 7. "[C]onstitutional interpretation has consistently recognized that the parents' claim to authority in their own household to direct the rearing of their children is basic in the structure of our society. 'It is cardinal with us that the custody, care and nurture of the child reside first in the parents, whose primary function and freedom include preparation for obligations the state can neither supply nor hinder.' " *Ibid.,* quoting *Prince* v. *Massachusetts, supra,* at 166. See *Wisconsin* v. *Yoder,* 406 U. S. 205, 231–233 (1972); *Pierce* v. *Society of Sisters,* 268 U. S. 510, 534–535 (1925); *Meyer* v. *Nebraska,* 262 U. S. 390, 399–401 (1923). Moreover, this statute would allow the State "to enquire into, prove, and punish," *Poe* v. *Ullman,* 367 U. S. 497, 548 (1961) (Harlan, J., dissenting), the exercise of this parental responsibility. The State points to no interest of sufficient magnitude to justify this direct interference with the parental guidance that is especially appropriate in this sensitive area of child development.[2]

---

[2] The particular provision at issue makes it a crime for "[a]ny person to sell or distribute any instrument or article, or any recipe, drug or medicine for the prevention of contraception to a minor under the age of sixteen years . . . ." Educ. Law § 6811 (8) (McKinney 1972). For the reasons stated in the text, this provision unjustifiably infringes the constitutionally protected interests of parents and married female minors, and it is invalid in those two respects. Although the prohibition on distribution might be sustained as to other individuals if the restrictions on

But in my view there is considerably more room for state regulation in this area than would be permissible under the plurality's opinion. It seems clear to me, for example, that the State would further a constitutionally permissible end if it encouraged adolescents to seek the advice and guidance of their parents before deciding whether to engage in sexual intercourse. *Planned Parenthood,* 428 U. S., at 91 (STEWART, J., concurring). The State justifiably may take note of the psychological pressures that might influence children at a time in their lives when they generally do not possess the maturity necessary to understand and control their responses. Participation in sexual intercourse at an early age may have both physical and psychological consequences. These include the risks of venereal disease and pregnancy, and the less obvious mental and emotional problems that may result from sexual activity by children. Moreover, society has long adhered to the view that sexual intercourse should not be engaged in promiscuously, a judgment that an adolescent may be less likely to heed than an adult.

Requiring minors to seek parental guidance would be consistent with our prior cases. In *Planned Parenthood,* we considered whether there was "any significant state interest in conditioning [a minor's] abortion [decision] on the consent of a parent or person *in loco parentis* that is not present in the case of an adult." 428 U. S., at 75. Observing that the minor necessarily would be consulting with a physician on all aspects of the abortion decision, we concluded that the Missouri requirement was invalid because it im-

---

parental distribution and distribution to married female minors could be treated as severable, the result "would be to create a program quite different from the one the legislature actually adopted." *Sloan* v. *Lemon,* 413 U. S. 825, 834 (1973). I therefore agree with the Court that the entire provision must be invalidated. See *Dorchy* v. *Kansas,* 264 U. S. 286, 291 (1924); *Dollar Co.* v. *Canadian C. & F. Co.,* 220 N. Y. 270, 279, 115 N. E. 711, 713 (1917).

posed "a special-consent provision, exercisable by a person other than the woman and her physician, as a prerequisite to a minor's termination of her pregnancy and [did] so without a sufficient justification for the restriction." *Ibid.* But we explicitly suggested that a materially different constitutional issue would be presented with respect to a statute assuring in most instances consultation between the parent and child. *Ibid.,* citing *Bellotti* v. *Baird,* 428 U. S. 132 (1976). See *Planned Parenthood, supra,* at 90–91 (STEWART, J., concurring).

A requirement of prior parental consultation is merely one illustration of permissible regulation in this area. As long as parental distribution is permitted, a State should have substantial latitude in regulating the distribution of contraceptives to minors.[3]

B

New York also makes it a crime for anyone other than a licensed pharmacist to sell or distribute contraceptives to adults and to minors aged 16 or over. The only serious justification offered by the State for this prohibition is that it is necessary to facilitate enforcement of the limitation on distribution to children under 16 years of age. Since the Court invalidates that limitation today, the pharmacy restriction lacks any rational justification. I therefore agree with the Court that § 6811 (8)'s limitation on the distribution of nonprescription contraceptives cannot be sustained.

But even if New York were to enact constitutionally permissible limitations on access for children, I doubt that it could justify the present pharmacy restriction as an enforcement measure. Restricting the kinds of retail outlets that may dis-

---

[3] As long as access is available through parents, I perceive no constitutional obstacle to state regulation that authorizes other designated adults—such as physicians—to provide relevant counseling.

tribute contraceptives may well be justified,[4] but the present statute even prohibits distribution by mail to adults.   In this respect, the statute works a significant invasion of the constitutionally protected privacy in decisions concerning sexual relations.   By requiring individuals to buy contraceptives over the counter, the statute heavily burdens constitutionally protected freedom.[5]

III

I also agree with the Court that New York cannot lawfully prohibit all "advertisement or display" of contraceptives. But it seems to me that the Court's opinion may be read too broadly.   It flatly dismisses, as justifications "classically" irrelevant, the State's contentions that the indiscriminate advertisement of contraceptive products in some settings could be unduly offensive and could be viewed by the young as legitimation of sexual promiscuity.   I agree that these jus-

---

[4] Absent some evidence that a restriction of outlets to registered pharmacists heavily burdens the constitutional interests of adults, there would be no basis for applying the standard of review articulated in *Griswold* and *Roe*. See Part I, *supra*. Indeed, in the absence of such evidence there would be no reason to set aside a legislative judgment that enforcement of constitutionally permissible limitations on access for minors, see Part II-A, *supra*, warrants a reasonable limitation on the means for marketing contraceptives. Without some limitations on the number and type of retail outlets it would be difficult—if not impossible—to effectuate the state interest in assuring that minors are counseled before purchasing contraceptive devices. As pharmacists are licensed professionals, the State may be justified in relying on them to act responsibly in observing regulations applicable to minors.

[5] It is not a satisfactory answer that an individual may preserve anonymity as one of a number of customers in a retail outlet. However impersonal the marketplace may be, it does not approach the privacy of the home. There may be some risk that mail distribution will occasionally permit circumvention of permissible restrictions with respect to children, but this does not justify the concomitant burden on the constitutional rights of adults.

tifications cannot support a complete ban on advertising, but I see no reason to cast any doubt on the authority of the State to impose carefully tailored restrictions designed to serve legitimate governmental concerns as to the effect of commercial advertising on the young.[6]

MR. JUSTICE STEVENS, concurring in part and concurring in the judgment.

For the reasons stated in Parts I, II, and III of the opinion of the Court, which I join, I agree that Population Planning Associates, Inc., has standing to challenge the New York statute and that the grant to licensed pharmacists of a monopoly in the distribution of nonmedical contraceptives is unconstitutional. I also agree with the conclusion that New York's prohibition against the distribution of contraceptives to persons under 16 years of age is unconstitutional, and with the Court's conclusion that the total suppression of advertising or display of contraceptives is invalid, but my reasons differ from those set forth in Part IV of MR. JUSTICE BREN-

---

[6] The State argues that unregulated commercial advertisement of contraceptive products would be viewed by the young as "legitimation" of— if not an open invitation to—sexual promiscuity. The Court simply finds on the basis of the advertisements in the record before us that this interest does not justify total suppression of advertising concerning contraceptives. The Court does leave open the question whether this or other state interests would justify regulation of the time, place, or manner of such commercial advertising. *Ante*, at 702 n. 29. In my view, such carefully tailored restrictions may be especially appropriate when advertising is accomplished by means of the electronic media. As Judge Leventhal recently observed in that context: "[T]here is a distinction between the all-out prohibition of a censor, and regulation of time and place of speaking out, which still leaves access to a substantial part of the mature audience. What is entitled to First Amendment protection is not necessarily entitled to First Amendment protection in all places. *Young* v. *American Mini Theatres, Inc.*, 427 U. S. 50 . . . (1976). Nor is it necessarily entitled to such protection at all times." *Pacifica Foundation* v. *FCC*, 181 U. S. App. D. C. 132, 157, 556 F. 2d 9, 34 (1977) (dissenting opinion).

NAN's opinion and I wish to add emphasis to the limitation on the Court's holding in Part V.

I

There are two reasons why I do not join Part IV. First, the holding in *Planned Parenthood of Missouri* v. *Danforth,* 428 U. S. 52, 72–75, that a minor's decision to abort her pregnancy may not be conditioned on parental consent, is not dispositive here. The options available to the already pregnant minor are fundamentally different from those available to nonpregnant minors. The former must bear a child unless she aborts; but persons in the latter category can and generally will avoid childbearing by abstention. Consequently, even if I had joined that part of *Planned Parenthood,* I could not agree that the Constitution provides the same measure of protection to the minor's right to use contraceptives as to the pregnant female's right to abort.

Second, I would not leave open the question whether there is a significant state interest in discouraging sexual activity among unmarried persons under 16 years of age. Indeed, I would describe as "frivolous" appellees' argument that a minor has the constitutional right to put contraceptives to their intended use, notwithstanding the combined objection of both parents and the State.

For the reasons explained by MR. JUSTICE POWELL, I agree that the statute may not be applied to married females between the ages of 14 and 16, or to distribution by parents. I am not persuaded, however, that these glaring defects alone justify an injunction against other applications of the statute. Only one of the three plaintiffs in this case is a parent who wishes to give contraceptives to his children. The others are an Episcopal minister who sponsors a program against venereal disease, and a mail-order firm, which presumably has no way to determine the age of its customers. I am satisfied, for the reasons that follow, that the statute is also invalid as applied to them.

The State's important interest in the welfare of its young citizens justifies a number of protective measures. See *Planned Parenthood of Central Missouri* v. *Danforth, supra,* at 102 (STEVENS, J., concurring in part and dissenting in part). Such special legislation is premised on the fact that young persons frequently make unwise choices with harmful consequences; the State may properly ameliorate those consequences by providing, for example, that a minor may not be required to honor his bargain. It is almost unprecedented, however, for a State to require that an ill-advised act by a minor give rise to greater risk of irreparable harm than a similar act by an adult.[1]

Common sense indicates that many young people will engage in sexual activity regardless of what the New York Legislature does; and further, that the incidence of venereal disease and premarital pregnancy is affected by the availability or unavailability of contraceptives. Although young persons theoretically may avoid those harms by practicing total abstention, inevitably many will not. The statutory prohibition denies them and their parents a choice which, if available, would reduce their exposure to disease or unwanted pregnancy.

---

[1] Only two other States have adopted similar legislation. Family Planning, Contraception and Voluntary Sterilization: An Analysis of Laws and Policies in the United States, Each State and Jurisdiction, A Report of the National Center for Family Planning Services 76 (1971) (DHEW Pub. No. (HSA) 74–16001). This publication contains a comprehensive survey of state laws in this area. The authors were aware of "no case in which either a doctor or a layman has been successfully prosecuted under any criminal statute for providing contraceptive information or services to a minor or has been held liable for damages for providing contraception to a minor without parental consent." *Id.,* at 70. This survey also indicated that "the clear trend is toward the removal of all such barriers to the sale and distribution of contraceptives." *Id.,* at 59. By 1971 there were 34 States with no law restricting or regulating distribution of contraceptives, *ibid.,* and 33 States with no restrictions on advertising or display. *Id.,* at 60.

The State's asserted justification is a desire to inhibit sexual conduct by minors under 16. Appellants do not seriously contend that if contraceptives are available, significant numbers of minors who now abstain from sex will cease abstaining because they will no longer fear pregnancy or disease.[2] Rather appellants' central argument is that the statute has the important *symbolic* effect of communicating disapproval of sexual activity by minors.[3] In essence, therefore, the statute is defended as a form of propaganda, rather than a regulation of behavior.[4]

Although the State may properly perform a teaching function, it seems to me that an attempt to persuade by inflicting harm on the listener is an unacceptable means of conveying a message that is otherwise legitimate. The propaganda technique used in this case significantly increases the risk of unwanted pregnancy and venereal disease. It is as though a State decided to dramatize its disapproval of motorcycles by forbidding the use of safety helmets. One need not posit a constitutional right to ride a motorcycle to characterize such a restriction as irrational and perverse.

Even as a regulation of behavior, such a statute would be defective. Assuming that the State could impose a uniform

---

[2] Appellants make this argument only once, in passing. See Brief for Appellants 20. In the District Court, appellants candidly admitted that "there is no evidence that teenage extramarital sexual activity increases in proportion to the availability of contraceptives. . . ." See 398 F. Supp. 321, 332. Indeed, appellants maintain that it is a "fact that youngsters will not use contraceptives even where available . . . ." Reply Brief for Appellants 5.

[3] The fact that the State admittedly has never brought a prosecution under the statute, id., at 2, is consistent with appellants' position that the purpose of the statute is merely symbolic.

[4] Appellants present no empirical evidence to support the conclusion that the State's "propaganda" is effective. Simply as a matter of common sense, it seems unlikely that many minors under 16 are influenced by the mere existence of a law indirectly disapproving of their conduct.

sanction upon young persons who risk self-inflicted harm by operating motorcycles, or by engaging in sexual activity, surely that sanction could not take the form of deliberately injuring the cyclist or infecting the promiscuous child. If such punishment may not be administered deliberately, after trial and a finding of guilt, it manifestly cannot be imposed by a legislature, indiscriminately and at random. This kind of government-mandated harm, is, in my judgment, appropriately characterized as a deprivation of liberty without due process of law.

II

In Part V of its opinion, the Court holds that New York's total ban on contraceptive advertising is unconstitutional under *Bigelow* v. *Virginia,* 421 U. S. 809, and *Virginia Pharmacy Bd.* v. *Virginia Citizens Consumer Council,* 425 U. S. 748. Specifically, the Court holds that all contraceptive advertising may not be suppressed because *some* advertising of that subject may be offensive and embarrassing to the reader or listener. I also agree with that holding.

The Court properly does not decide whether the State may impose any regulation on the content of contraceptive advertising in order to minimize its offensive character. I have joined Part V of the opinion on the understanding that it does not foreclose such regulation simply because an advertisement is within the zone protected by the First Amendment.

The fact that a type of communication is entitled to some constitutional protection does not require the conclusion that it is totally immune from regulation. Cf. *Young* v. *American Mini Theatres, Inc.,* 427 U. S. 50, 65–71 (opinion of STEVENS, J.). An editorial and an advertisement in the same newspaper may contain misleading matter in equal measure. Although each is a form of protected expression, one may be censored while the other may not.

In the area of commercial speech—as in the business of exhibiting motion pictures for profit—the offensive character of the communication is a factor which may affect the time, place, or manner in which it may be expressed. Cf. *Young* v. *American Mini Theatres, Inc., supra.* The fact that the advertising of a particular subject matter is *sometimes* offensive does not deprive all such advertising of First Amendment protection; but it is equally clear to me that the existence of such protection does not deprive the State of all power to regulate such advertising in order to minimize its offensiveness. A picture which may appropriately be included in an instruction book may be excluded from a billboard.

I concur in the judgment and in Parts I, II, III, and V of the Court's opinion.

MR. JUSTICE REHNQUIST, dissenting.

Those who valiantly but vainly defended the heights of Bunker Hill in 1775 made it possible that men such as James Madison might later sit in the first Congress and draft the Bill of Rights to the Constitution. The post-Civil War Congresses which drafted the Civil War Amendments to the Constitution could not have accomplished their task without the blood of brave men on both sides which was shed at Shiloh, Gettysburg, and Cold Harbor. If those responsible for these Amendments, by feats of valor or efforts of draftsmanship, could have lived to know that their efforts had enshrined in the Constitution the right of commercial vendors of contraceptives to peddle them to unmarried minors through such means as window displays and vending machines located in the men's room of truck stops, notwithstanding the considered judgment of the New York Legislature to the contrary, it is not difficult to imagine their reaction.[1]

---

[1] As well as striking down the New York prohibitions of commercial advertising and sales to persons under 16, the Court holds invalid the State's requirement that all sales be made by licensed pharmacists. Whatever New York's reasons for this particular restriction on distribution—and several can be imagined—I cannot believe that it could significantly impair

I do not believe that the cases discussed in the Court's opinion require any such result, but to debate the Court's treatment of the question on a case-by-case basis would concede more validity to the result reached by the Court than I am willing to do.[2] There comes a point when endless and ill-considered extension of principles originally formulated in quite different cases produces such an indefensible result that no logic chopping can possibly make the fallacy of the result more obvious. The Court here in effect holds that the First and Fourteenth Amendments not only guarantee full and free debate *before* a legislative judgment as to the moral dangers to which minors within the jurisdiction of the State should not be subjected, but goes further and absolutely prevents the representatives of the majority from carrying out such a policy *after* the issues have been fully aired.

No questions of religious belief, compelled allegiance to a secular creed, or decisions on the part of married couples as to procreation, are involved here. New York has simply decided that it wishes to discourage unmarried minors under 16 from having promiscuous sexual intercourse with one another. Even the Court would scarcely go so far as to say that this is not a subject with which the New York Legislature may properly concern itself.

That legislature has not chosen to deny to a pregnant woman, after the *fait accompli* of pregnancy, the one remedy

---

the access to these products of a person with a settled and deliberate intention to procure them.

[2] I cannot, however, let pass without comment, the statement that "the Court has not definitively answered the difficult question whether and to what extent the Constitution prohibits state statutes regulating [private consensual sexual] behavior among adults." *Ante,* at 688 n. 5, 694 n. 17. While we have not ruled on every conceivable regulation affecting such conduct the facial constitutional validity of criminal statutes prohibiting certain consensual acts has been "definitively" established. *Doe* v. *Commonwealth's Attorney,* 425 U. S. 901 (1976). See *Hicks* v. *Miranda,* 422 U. S. 332, 343–344 (1975).

which would enable her to terminate an unwanted pregnancy. It has instead sought to deter the conduct which will produce such *faits accomplis*.   The majority of New York's citizens are in effect told that however deeply they may be concerned about the problem of promiscuous sex and intercourse among unmarried teenagers, they may not adopt this means of dealing with it.   The Court holds that New York may not use its police power to legislate in the interests of its concept of the public morality as it pertains to minors.   The Court's denial of a power so fundamental to self-government must, in the long run, prove to be but a temporary departure from a wise and heretofore settled course of adjudication to the contrary. I would reverse the judgment of the District Court.

Index

supermajority and, 123–24
leakage problem, 121
minimum-driving-age: and public transportation, 156
minimum wage: for adolescents, 113–14
minor: as term, 86
minors: sexual behavior of, 10
Mnookin, Robert: 133n
Morris, Norval: xvi, xviii, 149
motion picture rating system: 130–31
motherhood: teenage, 158

Nazis: 56
neglected children: 53–54
New York City:
ethnic composition of, 158
and public transportation, 156
New York State:
pornography for minors, 8
prohibition of adolescent sexual behavior and contraceptive use, 62, 157
statutes relating to adolescence, 8
Nixon, Richard: 144

Oral Roberts University: 118–19

parens patriae: 31
parent: as term, 86
parental support: until age of majority, 6–7
Parham v. J.R., 442 U.S. 534 (1979): 77, 84–85, 88n, 108
"peer group": as term, 45
phasing strategy: 108–10
Planned Parenthood of Central Missouri v. Danforth, 428 U.S. 52 (1975): 99
Platt, Anthony M.: 47n
pornography: 8

Powell, Justice: dissent in *Goss,* 87n
pregnancy: of minor, 19–21, 65–68, 99
presumption of family liberty: 128–29
Price, R. F.: 97n
privacy rights:
of adolescents, 8
personal, 168
privileges:
phases of, 104
leakage of, 110
Progressive Era: public high school movement in, 91

Ralph, John H.: 46n
rebuttable presumption of liberty: 52, 108, 118, 138
regulation: state or parental, 108
Rehnquist, Justice: dissent in *Carey,* 9, 87n
Rendleman, Douglas: 46n
responsibility: 111–15
Robertson, Leon S.: 160n
Rosenheim, Margaret K.: 47n, 60n
Rubinson, Richard: 46n

Sands, Edward S.: 5
school suspensions: hearing requirements for, 83
Schlossman, Stephen: 46n, 75n
semi-autonomy: 123
jurisprudence of, 99–101
Sevareid, Eric: 61
sex education: for adolescents, 134
Silberman, Charles E.: 75n
Skokie, Illinois: 56
Skolnick, Arlene: 93, 97n
Smith College: 118–19
smokers lounge: 145–57
arguments against, 149–51